# KALAYA'S
# SOUTHERN THAI
# KITCHEN

## NOK SUNTARANON

### WITH NATALIE JESIONKA

PHOTOGRAPHS BY MICHAEL PERSICO
RECIPES EDITED BY PEGGY PAUL CASELLA

Clarkson Potter/
Publishers
*New York*

# CONTENTS

# INTRODUCTION

## You Find a Way to Keep Going

Growing up in Trang, Southern Thailand, we knew we were not rich, but life always had an element of brilliance to it, because the food my mother cooked was so delicious: perfect caramelized pork (see page 175), stir-fried eggplant (see page 180), Chinese Broccoli with Salted Fish (page 172), sour curry (see page 118). These foods offered moments of delight. In good times and in bad, my mom's food kept us going.

My mom, Kalaya, did not have an easy life. I'm writing this in Philadelphia, where I now live, where I run an award-winning restaurant named after her, which she has not been able to visit because her health makes it impossible to travel. She was orphaned early in life and worked as a domestic worker at the age of twelve, taking care of the kids of family friends. She didn't have much schooling, and she took care of those kids for a long time, teaching herself to cook and honing her skills in the kitchen.

When she married my dad, it wasn't always peaceful. His vices often forced my mom to make tough decisions. Like so many women around the world in difficult circumstances, she kept a strong face and kept herself together for her family. When we lost our house and my dad still brought friends over to the rental property, my mom cooked for them and was the most gracious host. She was generous even when we were really poor. She never said no, and she bought the best food, cooked the best food, and worked hard. And she would do the same the next day. My family does not dwell on the bad things that happen. We live for each day, and we move on.

We have to find a way forward and we look for the joy in life.

When my mom started her curry paste stall at our local market, Talat Yan Ta Khao, it was as much for stability as it was because she was good at it. I helped her peel ingredients and set up her curry stall from as early as I can remember. At five, I carried huge bricks of shrimp paste (which were almost as big as me) through the market for my mom. Did we play? I don't remember, but we did laugh a lot. It was my duty as a daughter and I was proud to do it. There was simply no other way.

Her curry stall grew popular and had many repeat customers. She was a staple of the market and people knew she used only the best ingredients for her pastes and sauces. She always smiled, always laughed.

As I grew older, she decided it would be best if I was to go to high school in Bangkok. She gave me the chance to live a life she never had. Without Kalaya, there would be no Nok. I owe her everything.

## You Will Learn to Cook

My husband always says I should learn to be more humble. Maybe he's right, but I am not humble about my food . . . yes, the food you are going to learn to cook from this book. My food reminds me of my beloved hometown, and of course of my mom. But my mom never taught me how to cook by holding my hand and telling me the steps.

I watched her cook and we enjoyed our conversations together. Watching her, I learned that you have to cook with your instinct. I never

really had to cook myself until I was an adult, working as a flight attendant. I was living in Kuwait with my colleagues and we wanted to make good Thai food. We were trying to use ingredients that were available to us there, or that we could bring back from Thailand in our suitcases. I think when you leave your mom's house and your country, this is how most people learn to cook. You miss the food of home and try to seek the comfort you remember.

I didn't have a chance to cook for my mom until much later. Every April, we would offer food to our ancestors for the Qingming festival and take care of their tombstones at the cemetery. We always looked forward to eating the mee tiaw and gai tom (noodles and steamed chicken) that my mother made. She would cook the noodles in lard, with cabbage, salt, and light seasoning, paired with steamed chicken and dipping sauces like Nam Jim Tao Jiew (page 33, Fermented Bean Sauce) or Nam Jim Waan (page 41, Sweet Chili Sauce). One year, she had surgery and couldn't cook for the festival. I took over and made the dish. My aunt said I made it taste just like my mom's cooking, which is the highest compliment.

## Cook Where You Are, with What You Have

At some point, I fell in love and moved to Philadelphia to be with my husband. By then, I was already well established in Bangkok, gaining seniority on my flight crew while also running a beloved Italian restaurant.

When I left Bangkok, I had to start my life over. For those first few months, I adjusted to American life. There weren't as many leisurely family meals, and everyone was always rushing. I had to learn to cook all over again with the ingredients available to me locally. It took a lot of trial and error, a lot of innovation, and many hours of work sometimes being thrown out. But

when I saw my family and my friends enjoyed my food, it created a lot of confidence in me. By then, I knew that I wanted food to be my career.

I went to a Western culinary school, and at home cooked for my friends and neighbors. I worked in a bakery for a few months, and then joined the catering business of a famous chef. I love a good flaky pastry with my coffee, but I missed the fiery and inspiring flavors of Southern Thailand. Much of the food I was learning about and was asked to cook felt one-dimensional. At home, I was cooking my mom's food and the food from my memory while improvising. The way I made my green curry (see page 127) with extra basil at the end to maintain the green brightness and avoid oxidation was a recipe I developed in Philly. I would make chicken soup with bitter melon or a luxurious oxtail soup that I remembered my mom making me when I was sick. It was not without its complications. One day I needed lemongrass. I went to my neighborhood grocery store. The only option they had was one 3-inch stick of lemongrass in a plastic box. At that moment, I missed the abundant produce markets of my childhood and how we could get foot-long beautiful bunches of lemongrass to use for two weeks.

Over the years, I found a butcher, my favorite produce market, and a fishmonger, and now I know the exact places to get the best-quality ingredients for my recipes, but it took me a while to build my network. Those first few years I worked with what I could access, and I found ways to make my food just as good as back home. In this spirit of discovery, I never felt discouraged. I kept working until I got it right.

## You Have to Take the Chance

I love Philadelphia. It is a city that always has room to embrace creativity and grit. You can be unknown one day, and the next day if you do something interesting, funny, or innovative, the city will celebrate it, even if it's climbing to the top of a greasy telephone pole or making a football field–size banh mi hoagie like we did for the Super Bowl. It was also Philadelphia diners who embraced my food when I started a small thirty-seat restaurant in my Queen Village neighborhood. The restaurant was just a dream, I didn't even know I would secure the space when I handed over the deposit. I was a Thai woman, a new American, and someone who was unknown to the Philadelphia restaurant scene. I felt an urgency to preserve true Southern Thai recipes, and I wanted to share the delicious and vibrant food of my childhood.

I served Southern-Style Crab Curry (page 117, Gaeng Pu)—with really big chunks of crab— Tom Yum Goong (page 150, Hot and Sour Thai Soup with Shrimp) with giant river prawns practically climbing out of the soup, Southern-Style Chicken Curry (page 114, Gaeng Gai Khao Mun) with Green Coconut Rice (page 235), and intricate dumplings shaped like flowers made purple from the butterfly pea flower and stuffed with pork. I cooked with my heart, and instinct, just like I remembered the way my mom cooked for me. That first year, we were voted restaurant

of the year by Philadelphia's top food critics and by *Esquire* magazine. Since then, I never stopped, I never hesitated, I just kept working, kept going, just like my mom.

In 2022 we opened a 130-seat restaurant in the Fishtown neighborhood of Philadelphia, and life has been crazy ever since. In 2023, I won the James Beard Award, and we were honored as one of the top 50 restaurants in America by the *New York Times*. If you asked me ten years ago would I be here, I would have smiled and said it's my dream. Now it's my life, and every day I get to showcase my food and share it with the world.

## What Is True Thai Food?

Every so often, a customer will try to tell me about my food. They will say, "This is not Thai food," or my favorite, "I have been to Thailand, and this food is not like what I had in Thailand." When I hear this, I take a breath, I smile. I look them in the eyes and ask what they ate in Thailand. Sometimes it's because they didn't go to the South, and they're not familiar with our cuisine. But usually, what they remember is some version of pad Thai, or red curry served at a restaurant catering to farang (our endearing term for foreigners, which is anyone who is not Thai). Those curries are often watered down and sweetened.

The food I cook is the food of my childhood and of my memories in Southern Thailand, and it is the product of my experiences as a child helping at my mom's curry stall, a flight attendant traveling the world, an Italian restaurant owner, and a housewife. Now I am a chef. In a lifetime you can be so many things, and as my career as a chef launched, my goal was to share some of the most honest and elevated Thai food America has to offer. What I serve may be new to you, and that's why it can be so thrilling to come to the restaurant.

It's hard to make people get out of their comfort zone when it comes to Thai food. To be honest, the super-sweet sticky noodles that have passed as pad Thai in North America are nothing like the pad Thai we have at home. Nowadays, it's even hard to find good pad Thai in Thailand. But I have to ask myself, why do so many people only know pad Thai and not a warm and fragrant Khao Mok Gai (page 69, Morning Market Chicken Biryani) or a sweet-peppery Goong Ob Woonsen (page 223, Baked Shrimp with Glass Noodles)?

When my customers used to ask me why I don't serve pad Thai all the time, I say, "It's because I don't have a couch for you to eat cheap takeout and watch TV on." If the only thing I ate when I went to an Italian restaurant was spaghetti, my life would feel sad. I would be limiting myself and my ability to experience new flavors and ideas. Imagine how much you will miss out when you expect only pad Thai for the rest of your lifetime. It would be a gastronomic tragedy.

But more recently, I have started serving a high-quality pad Thai. Maybe I am mellowing out. But now I find it's a good entry point for people who feel intimidated by new experiences. Maybe this time they will try the pad Thai and they feel comfortable enough to try the Kanom Jeen (page 65, Rice Noodles with Coconut Fish Curry) or the fragrant, calming Soup Hang Wua (page 157, Oxtail Soup with Herbs and Crispy Shallots) alongside it. The other day a lady told me, "This is not pad Thai, this is so much better than that," and I bet next time, she will feel anchored enough to try more exciting things on the menu.

But what is real Thai food? Ask chefs in Bangkok, they may tell you about the influence of international flavors and innovation. In Chiang Rai, they may tell you about how important it is to use their traditional techniques. And if you asked my mom in Trang, she would say, "It's the food I decided to cook that day."

I will always challenge the stereotype that Thai food is nothing but cheap takeout; our cuisine can be affordable and quick, and it can be highly refined—we have a long tradition of royal cuisine as well as street food. And our different regions are proud of their own cuisines—the lime juice/fish sauce/toasted rice/meat larb from the Northeast, served with Sticky Rice (page 236), is iconic, as are the fermented soybean dishes of the North.

On the Southern Thai table, there are as many as fifteen dishes served together, all with a unique layer of flavors and complexity, and the freshest ingredients from the farm, garden, and sea. Our cuisine is often spicier, tangier, more coconut-rich, and more influenced by Indian, Chinese, and Malay cultures. But I will also challenge the idea that "authentic" Thai food means that the different regions eat only their regional specialties. When I was growing up, yes, we loved our Southern Thai dishes, but we also loved larb and dishes from other regions, and that is part of my food story—and a part of this cookbook. We love food so much in Thailand and there is such a fabulous range of foods, it's hard to watch when people limit themselves.

Also, Thailand has a rich beautiful history of travelers, traders, and epic kingdoms. Our stories are woven from the tapestry of our strength and our values; from ghost stories that teach life lessons and amazing battles between elephants and snakes and tigers that save the world. In this book, I am happy to be able to share my stories, food, and techniques. You will taste history in the recipes, but it will be of my family and my memory, and while I will always honor the rich history of my country, all of these recipes are deeply personal. And look, I'm not here to teach you the history of Thailand, just like I don't expect anyone to teach me the history of America when I eat a salted brownie.

## Nok's Way

The Southern Thai food I cook, and the food of my family, is joyful, beautiful, and brings people together. The Southern Thai table can be a one-plate meal, but our meals are usually meant to be served family-style. The complete meal is a collection of dishes that feature flavors and cooking techniques that accompany each other: a bright and beautiful curry, a timeless stir-fry, a surprising soup, and a colorful steamed dish, combined with accompanying sauces and dips.

Don't be intimidated; you don't *have* to cook everything every time. And I recommend you get ahead: Prepping some sauces and flavorful pastes and marinades is key; with them safely in your fridge, you can throw together a meal quickly anytime. If you start cooking with a few recipes in mind each time, you will be able to master the Southern Thai table with elegance and grace. The kitchen is your runway.

You bought this book so you can cook real Southern Thai food and make spectacular meals that make you feel alive with every bite. You will discover incredible happiness when you follow the recipes exactly, and you will develop a foundational understanding of what Southern Thai food should be: spicy, tangy, bold, earthy, herbaceous, and sweet.

The ingredients in these recipes are abundant, often packed with herbs and spices. When you hesitate, when you have doubt, when you say, "But, Nok, that's so much black pepper! But, Nok, do you really want me to use that much cilantro?" I will smile at you and say, "Yes, that is exactly how it should be." I approach my food like I approach shopping—both for food and for clothes: without hesitation.

If you've never visited Southern Thailand, or my restaurant in Philadelphia, you need to know where to start—and you will need to do it my way first.

Trust me, trust the process. Make these recipes as written the first time, so you taste them the way I want you to taste them. Then from there, feel free to change them to suit you, if need be. You'll see that I was right. (Just kidding! Kind of.)

## No Spice Modifications, No Apologies!

One thing I do have to emphasize, because so many people have tried to tell me to change my spice level: Southern Thai food is some of the spiciest in Thailand, and I serve my food the way it should be, but that doesn't mean my food is "too spicy," either. First, not everything we serve is hot. Did I mention we have a lot of range in our food? Second, the chili heat from these dishes is complex; it can be sweet and fruity, or smoky and nutty with different intensities, so don't judge it right away. The fresh ingredients and herbs in the food complement one another so you can taste complex layers of flavor. Nobody is going to die from chilies. And your life will be happier because of it, so use the correct amount when cooking with this book. Would I tell you how to cook your hamburger or mac and cheese without tasting it? No. So again, try it my way first, please.

I understand that sometimes it might be harder to find some of my ingredients, or these ingredients might be new to you, and that's part of the adventure of cooking my food. Most ingredients that you cannot find in the store can be purchased online, and I offer more common substitutions for some of them. I don't think substitutions are bad; remember, that is how I cooked this food for much of my life when I wasn't in Thailand. But for ingredients that might be unfamiliar to you, embrace them and you will find a lot of joy in learning something new. I want you to make my recipes until you feel comfortable, understand the true flavors, and then you can start adapting and experimenting for your own Thai home cooking.

# THE EQUIPMENT YOU'LL NEED

In Thailand, a kitchen can be two small burners over a gas tank or a charcoal grill. Whether you have a big chef's kitchen or one burner, you can make most of my food. Getting your kitchen ready is not too big of an investment. Most recipes can be made in a cast-iron skillet, Dutch oven, or frying pan unless there is a specific call for a wok (sometimes there is, you just can't get that quick-heat cooking any other way). While I love cookware that will last a lifetime, you don't need anything too fancy. I have a mix of custom- and artisan-made equipment like my chef's knives, and inexpensive pieces from the restaurant store like a steamer rack. I have cooked these recipes in kitchens around the world. My mom cooked on a simple single high-heat burner and made the best food. You don't need a lot. What you really need to cook good food is focus and determination, and a little technique. Here is a list of equipment that would be helpful for the recipes in this book.

## A VERY GOOD AND SHARP KNIFE

You would be surprised at how many people in America cook with dull knives and how it slows them down. Having sharp knives around will change the way you cook. It needs to be so sharp that when you cut your finger, the cut will be clean, and it will heal easier, too. You can get a cheap sharpener and that should do the trick.

## ELECTRIC SPICE GRINDER

This piece of equipment will grind your spice blends finely and evenly and save hours compared to doing it the old way, with a mortar and pestle. Do it the old way once so you satisfy your curiosity; then you will be even more grateful for a spice grinder.

## MORTAR AND PESTLE

If you *must* do it the old way, get a stone mortar and pestle where the spices won't jump out. A heavier mortar and pestle is more effective. You want finely ground spices, so put on your favorite playlist and get to work. When you feel ready to give up, use an electric spice grinder.

## CAST-IRON SKILLET

When you get your cast-iron skillet hot enough, that is when the magic happens. You can use a cast-iron skillet unless I specifically mention only using a wok. Keep it clean and keep it seasoned and you should be good to go.

## WOK

A hot wok is a powerhouse and cooks food beautifully. There are times you will need the heat to fry and steam the food in a way that only a wok can deliver, and it's useful for stir-fries. The wok doesn't need to be fancy; you just need to get it hot and smoking and all will fall into place.

## NONSTICK PANS

Nonstick pans are the best thing that can happen to anyone. You probably have these around, and they do come in handy for preparing garlic oils, toasting spices, flipping omelets, and so much more. You don't need the pretty Instagram pans, just one where the coating will last and you make them work for you.

## A 10- TO 12-INCH STEAMER POT OR STEAMER RACK

The range of steamers is amazing; from tiered steamers to small steamer baskets. This will be useful for recipes like fish, dumplings, and steamed meats. Metal steamers will last longer.

## CITRUS JUICER

This will make your life easier when you need to squeeze fresh limes.

## BLENDER

A good blender will make your curry pastes fast and easy. Make sure it's strong enough so the motor will last through years of making curry paste.

## FOOD PROCESSOR

This is great for curry pastes and for when we make mixtures with protein. You can make big batches and freeze the leftovers.

## DUTCH OVEN

A good Dutch oven is great for braises, bakes, curries, and soups. Also in many of the stir-fry recipes, you can use a heavy Dutch oven instead of a wok if that's what you have.

## STOCKPOT

There is nothing like having a stockpot of Thai soup boiling on the stove. Get a big stockpot (8 quarts is good), because you will want to make a lot of stock and soups from my recipes.

## GRILL

I use my gas grill outside, but any grill is fine. A charcoal grill can impart beautiful flavor. Just know that each kind of grill has a different kind of heat, so cooking times will vary. I want you always to trust your senses and read the descriptions in the recipes, not just go by the suggested times, but this is especially true if you are using a grill.

# THE SOUTHERN THAI PANTRY

My mother used only the freshest of ingredients in her curry pastes. She knew how to tell the sharpest spices, the punchiest herbs, and the best quality of shrimp paste. If a vendor offered her a superior product, she would cultivate that relationship and always go back to them. If a vendor cheated her with the weight of the product or quality of the spices, she would never use them again.

Just like my mom, I won't settle for anything less than the best, and you shouldn't either. But that doesn't mean you should be intimidated when building your Thai pantry. In Trang, we source ingredients directly from our home gardens. There are gardens growing along fences in the front of our houses where you can pick herbs and ingredients like holy basil, curry leaves, and lemongrass. Our coconuts come directly from the trees around us, and if you can't grow it yourself, someone will sell it at the market from their home garden.

I understand that home cooks are concerned they may need dozens of unfamiliar ingredients, but you don't need your own garden, and Southern Thai ingredients are easy to find at any Asian grocer, and online in a pinch. When you can, have fun with it; and search for the freshest ingredients at the farmers' markets or supermarkets that are available to you. When you cannot, use what is accessible and the recipes will still be really good. If you can't find fresh galangal (which is not surprising), the frozen works, and is often more consistent anyway.

I can't lie about this—some of the ingredients that I remember just aren't the same here. And that is okay! When I came to America, I used whatever green chilies I could find, and it was a matter of learning and tasting the ingredients, in order to know what works and what you like. When I cook here, I try to use the skill my mom had, listening to the ingredients I have and adjusting to still make the food delicious. If the ingredients are new to you, but you find that you like them, then that is all that matters.

Here are some of the key ingredients in these recipes and, if you have different options, how to make sure you are getting the good ones.

## Fresh Herbs & Produce

### TURMERIC ROOT
Turmeric is a rhizome that grows abundantly in Southern Thailand and adds an earthy bitterness to curry pastes, as well as a bright yellow color. Using fresh turmeric is key in curry pastes for a beautiful color and flavor combination. In most cases, you can substitute organic turmeric powder for fresh turmeric, but the ground turmeric has to be pure so the flavor will be more intense and it will have a similar impact.

### MAKRUT LIME LEAF
Makrut lime leaf is citrusy and floral and helps add an aromatic tanginess to curry pastes. We use makrut lime zest in Thailand, but the fruit can be difficult to find; it's easier to find fresh or frozen lime leaf in North America. I chiffonade these often, as tearing them or smashing them helps release flavor. These are also often called kaffir lime leaves, but we are moving away from that term since it is offensive.

## GALANGAL

Galangal is grown all over Southern Thailand and is both delicate and has a bite at the same time. Galangal looks somewhat similar to ginger but has notes of citrus and pepper and is essential to bring out heat and herbal flavor in curry pastes. Finding fresh galangal is possible, but it is woody in America, so I prefer to use the frozen because it is light and easier to find, and it's softer to use in the food processor. When you buy galangal fresh, you will likely get a pound. Clean them, cut them small, and freeze them, so whenever you need it you can have it all year.

## LEMONGRASS

Lemongrass has a citrusy, minty cooling punch; when the stems are smashed, lemongrass releases an oil that brightens curry pastes. If you can't find fresh lemongrass, frozen minced lemongrass is available at Asian grocery stores, but dried lemongrass will not work for my recipes.

### How to Prep Lemongrass

Cut off the very bottom of the lemongrass stalk if there is a root end and take off the outer tough, dry leaves, until you get to the ones that are smooth and fresh. Sometimes lemongrass is smashed, sometimes it's tied in a knot, and sometimes it is chopped; follow the instructions in the recipe and you will impart the maximum flavor. If the recipe is for minced lemongrass, to be eaten (instead of infused and taken out), thinly slice and mince only the white and very light green colored parts.

## THAI BASIL

In Thailand we use many types of basil, but for my recipes, there are Siam basil (what most people here just called Thai basil) and krapao, also known as holy basil, which offer different flavors. But use whatever basil you can get your hands on. We often use basil as a green, meaning almost like a vegetable, not just one leaf on top, and that creates a wonderful and robust balance in the recipe. Holy basil has the flavor of pepper, licorice, and mint and is grown in neighborhood gardens throughout Trang. This gives curry paste its herbaceous flavor. Depending on the basil, the flavors might be sweet, spicy, or mellow; but don't stress, all of it will be delicious.

## CURRY LEAF

Curry leaves are very aromatic, musky and peppery. They add a savory depth to Southern Thai curry pastes. Fresh or dry curry leaves will work for any of these recipes. They can be found at Asian grocery stores in the produce section or in the frozen section, or ordered online.

## CILANTRO

In Thailand we *pak chee roye na*, "top with cilantro," in so many dishes. Always give cilantro a chance. It adds a cooling brightness to most spicy dishes and is key in so many of our recipes. Long live cilantro.

## CULANTRO

It's time to expand your knowledge of herbs. This is not a typo. Culantro (prounouced *kul-antro*) is different from cilantro, even though the flavor is related. Culantro is a bold citrusy herb that has small sawtooth-edged leaves (sometimes called saw-tooth coriander). Culantro goes by many names. In Thailand we call it "phak chi farang." You may also find it called shado beni, recao, or ngò gai. Culantro can withstand long cooking times.

## SATOR BEAN

This is also known as stink bean, but they aren't really that stinky. They have a little bit of a garlic or onion funkiness. Use frozen sator beans and make your life easy.

## Spices

### BLACK PEPPER
In Southern Thailand, we used black pepper to add heat before chilies were accessible. Black pepper in curry paste adds a sharp bold heat. What makes the difference in many of our dishes is pepper, and our generous use of it. Good black pepper should be sharp and have a flavor that lingers. In Thai cooking, black pepper does not need to be freshly ground, but the fresher the better, and use organic if you can.

### WHITE PEPPER
White pepper is stronger and more vibrant than black pepper. It is sharper and has a hot, grassy, and fermented taste that adds a kick to Southern Thai curry pastes. In my hometown of Trang, we use white pepper often, because its brightness matches well with seafood, which we love.

### GROUND TURMERIC
Turmeric adds an earthy mellowness to recipes and a beautiful color. Look for organic turmeric, as you want the least amount of filler.

### CINNAMON
Always have cinnamon sticks and ground cinnamon on hand. One stick of cinnamon can add so much warming depth to braises and soups.

### STAR ANISE
Star anise is toasty and warming and very fragrant. It has a very sweet aroma, and a little bit of licorice, too. It stands out in soups, curries, and rice recipes. (Note that star anise is very different from anise.) Star anise is sold in starlike pods, though sometimes they can be broken up in the bag.

### CUMIN
Cumin whole or ground is earthy and musky.

### NUTMEG
In Trang, the fresh nutmeg is the pit of a fruit that is our local delicacy. We make curry, we make juice, we season water with it, or we candy it.

### MACE
Mace is both mellow and peppery and adds a subtle sweetness to recipes. It is actually the outer layer of nutmeg, so they have related flavors.

#### To Toast and Grind Your Own Spices
Working one spice at a time, toast the whole seeds or pods in a dry skillet over medium heat. Stand nearby and pay attention, stirring or tossing occasionally. First, you will hear little cracking sounds and smell the spice's aroma. Then a few seeds will begin to dance in the pan. As soon as there is dancing, they're ready; pour them into a mortar or bowl. Repeat with the next spice. Grind the toasted seeds or pods with a pestle or in a spice grinder. Freshly ground spices are most flavorful when used right away, but you can keep them in an airtight container in the pantry (just let them cool completely before storing). They will keep their flavor for a few weeks.

### TOASTED RICE POWDER
This is not really a spice, but Thai cooks use it to add a fragrant texture element to certain dishes. It's not easy to find in stores, but is easy to make at home.

#### To Make Toasted Rice Powder
Take ½ cup raw sticky rice (aka sweet or glutinous rice) and toast it in a small heavy saucepan over high heat, stirring frequently, until the rice starts to turn golden brown. Reduce the heat to medium, and when you see a lot of browning, stir rapidly until all of the rice is a toasty light brown color. This whole process should take 6 to 10 minutes.

Remove the pan from the heat and spread the rice on a clean kitchen towel or plate to cool.

Transfer the toasted rice to a spice grinder or food processor and grind to a coarse powder. Let cool and use; store the leftovers in an airtight container. It will keep forever, but you can refresh its flavor by toasting it for a little bit before using.

## CHILIES

Did you know chilies are fruits? They add a beautiful aroma, clean heat, and balance to recipes that are sweet or sour and create a vibrant bite. Follow the recipe, trust me on the quantity of chilies, and don't touch your eyes while chopping them. Please and thank you.

## FRESH OR FROZEN THAI CHILIES

Thai chilies, also called bird's-eye chilies or Thai bird chilies, add a clean heat that is different from dried chilies or pepper flakes. If you can't find fresh Thai chilies, you can use frozen chilies and thaw them whenever you need.

## DRIED CHILIES

Dried chilies add a heat and fruitiness to Southern Thai curry pastes and can offer warm toasty flavors.

## PANDAN LEAVES

Dinner or dessert, pandan leaves can be so many things to your recipe. If coconut and grassy vanilla had a baby, this would be it. We use it for curry pastes, curries, soups, desserts and so much more. It's both mellow and sweet. Fresh or frozen pandan work for any of these recipes.

## Thai Sauces

## FISH SAUCE

I am not married to any brand, so use the best one you can find. What I recommend is tasting it; it will be salty, but if you taste a few different ones, you will find out which are too salty. It should have a strong taste, but also a lot of depth.

## FERMENTED SOYBEAN PASTE (TAO JIEW)

A savory paste of fermented beans, like a cousin of miso. Look for a Thai brand, or if you're using white miso as a substitute, look at the label and make sure you find a reduced-sodium version, or the lowest sodium version if you're choosing from several options.

## THAI BLACK SOY SAUCE

This is usually gluten-free, and again, not that many brands have different flavors. It's soy sauce that is sweetened and the texture is thicker than regular soy sauce. Be sure this is a Thai brand, or at least that it has a sweetener in the ingredients.

## GOLDEN MOUNTAIN SEASONING SAUCE

Each region in Thailand has their own soy sauce. In Trang we use locally made soy sauce. "Seasoning sauce" is a soy sauce that has been preseasoned, so it is sweeter and has extra umami; we often use it for stir-fries. Any gluten-free Thai seasoning sauce will work here.

## OYSTER SAUCE

Though we use this rarely, it's a good item to have in the pantry. It's a dark, thick soy-based sauce that has the flavor of cooked oysters. Gluten-free oyster sauce is usually optional, and if you have a shellfish allergy, you can look for a vegetarian version.

## Canned or Packaged Items

## DIAMOND CRYSTAL KOSHER SALT

I use Diamond Crystal kosher salt. I encourage you to use Diamond Crystal anywhere in the recipes that call for kosher salt otherwise the recipe will come out off-balance. If you cannot find Diamond Crystal, you can use other brands, but reduce the amount of salt by a third. For example, use 2 teaspoons of salt for every 1 tablespoon (3 teaspoons) Diamond Crystal.

## COCONUT MILK

We use a lot of coconut milk in the South. Try to find a Thai brand of canned coconut milk. (It will say made or produced in Thailand.) Coconut milk is also packed in larger 16-ounce cartons that must be refrigerated after opening.

## COCONUT CREAM

This is the really decadent part of the coconut and makes recipes rich and creamy. If you don't have coconut cream, you can always take coconut milk and reduce it on the stove to make it extra creamy, but this can be found easily at most grocery stores. Just make sure you're not buying the sweetened stuff meant for piña coladas. The coconut cream I use has no sugar.

## PALM SUGAR

Palm sugar is the sugar derived from the sap of a palm tree, and adds a natural complex sweetness to certain dishes. You may see this labeled as coconut palm sugar, and that is fine, too. You can find it at any Asian grocery or order it online. It comes in small discs, large discs, and a paste that involves some labor to scrape out of the jar. Working with palm sugar takes some patience, as it won't dissolve right away. If you are in a bind, you can always use brown sugar, though it won't be quite the same.

## PICKLED MUSTARD GREENS

Pickled mustard greens are versatile and add a sour/mellow tartness to complement eggs or protein. You can boil them or soak them in the fridge overnight to remove the salt. We make our own pickled mustard greens in Thailand, but the packaged ones are very consistent.

## THAI TAMARIND CONCENTRATE

When I do my grocery shopping, I want my life to be easy. Tamarind concentrate is your sour sweet friend and helps give dipping sauces and sour curries that punch. I use Thai brands of pure tamarind concentrate because it has the right consistency. When you are looking for pure tamarind concentrate, the first ingredient should be tamarind. There are some mysterious tamarind sauces in Western grocery stores where the first ingredient is soy sauce. Do not use these! Tamarind concentrate is widely available and makes all the difference in flavor for dipping sauces. Be sure, though, that you are getting tamarind "concentrate" and not "paste" or "pulp." In the old days, we would buy a large block of tamarind pulp with the seeds, pour hot water over the block, soak it, hand-mix it, and strain it. You can still do that, then measure what comes out of the sieve. But now, why go through the pain? Whatever you do, please don't get full tamarind fruit and try to make pulp yourself. You like your time and energy. Use it on self-care and don't try to make tamarind concentrate yourself.

## JUMBO LUMP CRABMEAT

I know what you're thinking: Why is she talking about crabmeat in the part of the book that is about pantry ingredients? Well, it's because I think it is a good idea to keep good-quality canned or packaged crabmeat in the refrigerator at all times; usually it will last for many months. You can also make so many delicious meals with it. The larger the lumps, the better.

Yes, it is expensive, but you deserve luxury once in a while, and you will find how easy it is to cook with straight out of the package (would you want to clean and pick that crabmeat yourself?), and the flavorful final recipes are worth it. Keep it stocked and thank me later.

## Dried Ingredients (Including Rice & Noodles)

### SHRIMP PASTE

Shrimp paste, known as kapi in Thailand, gets better with age. It's a firm paste made of salted krill, and it adds a strong feeling of umami and funk to curry pastes and sauces. We have our own unique shrimp paste in the South, where it first originated. It's pungent and sweet and delicious.

### DRIED SHRIMP

For dried shrimp, the better-quality ones are more briny and savory in flavor, and should not have a strong fishy smell. Some of the cheaper ones can be overly salty, so finding a midrange dried shrimp should do the trick. Salt levels may be subjective, but remember in many recipes it is our source of saltiness. But use what you can find at the Asian grocery store. Taste it after it is open and put in the freezer and it can be stored for a long time.

### DRIED MUSHROOMS

Find nice, beautiful plump dried shiitakes. These are easily available at the Asian grocery store and can be reconstituted by soaking for a few hours.

**To Prep Dried Shiitakes**

Put the dried shiitake mushrooms in a medium bowl and pour in 4 cups water. Cover and let the mushrooms soak in the refrigerator overnight. If you're in a hurry, put them in a medium pot with 4 cups water, keep them submerged with a heatproof bowl, and bring to a boil. As soon as it boils, turn off the heat and let them steep for 30 minutes. Depending on the recipe, you will save the soaking water to use later in the recipe or you can save for another use (or discard).

### SALTED EGG YOLK

Cured egg yolks can add a lot of flavors and they can be used in a number of recipes. It's always good to have a package on hand. Also save your time and please don't try to make them yourself.

### DRIED ANCHOVIES

Anchovies are healthy, shiny, and packed with umami. We use these for flavor and for beauty in our salads. Quality can be subjective and there is a range of prices for anchovies, but you should be fine with a middle price point. Use what is available to you.

### GLASS NOODLES

Glass noodles are quick-cooking noodles that soak up flavor beautifully and have a bouncy texture. They are made usually of mung bean starch, not rice. Prepare according to the package directions, as soaking and cooking time vary.

### RICE NOODLES

These days you can find rice vermicelli noodles (sen mee) almost anywhere. These are round, different from the wide rice sticks (sen lek) used for pad Thai. They are gluten-free. Prepare according to the package directions.

### THAI JASMINE RICE

Jasmine rice is subtly fragrant comfort. It's so much more than plain white rice, and well-cooked rice can make a meal. I don't care get if you get the twenty-pound bag at your bulk store or a small bag at your corner store, always keep this stocked.

### STICKY RICE

Depending on the packaging, this is often called sweet rice or glutinous rice, and has the color of chalk; it is not glassy like other rice grains. Thai sticky rice is firm and has a bounce in the chew. For many grilled dishes it is meant to be eaten with your hands and used as a utensil to combine with a bite of protein like grilled chicken or vegetables and dipping sauce. Just know that it's not cooked like regular rice; we use a process where we soak it in water, and then steam it in a steamer.

# A FEW MORE THOUGHTS BEFORE WE BEGIN

### It's Not Too Many Chilies!

You are losing sleep over the amount of chilies again. Why? It may feel out of your comfort zone, but I will be honest with you, there is no five-elephant-spice BS here. The reason you might feel afraid of spice is because you are used to cheap Thai takeout that doesn't use real chilies at all. They use tablespoons of poor-quality red pepper flakes. The stuff you put on your pizza is not a garnish for Thai food!

To be honest, I think that for early immigrants who opened Thai restaurants, the business owners may have been afraid they would not succeed if they didn't adjust heat and sugar for a new audience. Then everyone became afraid of spice.

When people say, "I don't eat spicy food," or "I can't handle spicy food," it's not true. You must believe in yourself, and you must eat the food right. Use real ingredients and balance the flavors on the table with sweetness and sour, bitter and cream that cut through the spice. Feel the fear and do it anyway. You will be better for it and really start enjoying your food.

### Embrace Imperfect Fruits & Vegetables

Do you love zero-waste living? Embrace eating like Southern Thai people and discover the possibilities of unripe and overripe fruits and vegetables. At the market in Trang, a curry vendor cut young jackfruit that fell off the tree. She knew how to handle it in a special way to preserve the flavor and the fruit. The jackfruit was meaty, bitter, and delicious. We don't discard the produce that falls off the tree or is overripe, for there is always something to do with it! With young bananas, we make curry; with overripe bananas, we make jam. Don't underestimate the power of youth or graceful aging for your produce.

### No Chopsticks, No Knives

We don't eat Thai food with chopsticks unless it's a noodle soup. I don't know why American Thai restaurants encourage the use of chopsticks, but it's not how we eat. Our fork is used to gently shovel the food on the spoon and we eat with our spoons. We do not use knives. Every bite of a Thai meal should be a bite-size spoonful.

### Do You Really Want to Do It the Old Way?

While I grew up using a mortar and pestle, and then eventually a very large grinder, the method you choose to grind spices will still preserve the integrity of the ingredients and the flavors. There are only a few recipes that call for a mortar and pestle. When it is not required, make your life easier and use a grinder. If you must devote your time and energy to pounding your spices, then be sure your mortar and pestle has a wide brim and is deep. In this era, you don't need to use a mortar and pestle, but if you want to, you can. I admire your commitment. Just use the method that makes you the happiest.

## Cleaning Up

When I was young, it was my job to help my mom prepare ingredients, pound spices, and set up the curry stall before school. After school, we would help her clean up the stall and prepare for the next day before she cooked dinner. For the next day to go smoothly, everything would need to be spotless and ready to go for the early morning. We didn't dread it; it was something we always just had to do (and we did not have a modern dishwasher). At the restaurant I have a team to help me, but at home, when I'm cooking dinner for my family or a dinner party, I still stay up after everyone leaves and do the dishes for the next day.

I know what it's like to be in the kitchen after a long day of cooking, once everyone has enjoyed themselves and a giant pile of dishes is staring back at you. In this book, there are recipes for one-pot or one-wok meals, and you can think about your ingredient prep as part of the cleanup equation: a cutting board plus your compost plus your pot. Some recipes, such as omelets, require two pans and a plate or two to get the technique right. The easiest way to tackle this is to have a plan. Make the curry pastes and dips first—you can make them days or even weeks before—and have them in the fridge ready to cook throughout the week. Once the foundational pastes and sauces are ready, you will be surprised at how quick things come together and how cleanup will be under control. If you are throwing a Southern Thai dinner party, try tackling each set of dishes after the recipe is complete, or you can always enlist your kids or family or friends to help wash and dry. If you live alone, a favorite podcast and your dishwasher can keep you company. Dirty dishes can seem infinite and endless, especially when you are busy, but you are not alone, and you can feel accomplished knowing you have cooked beautiful food.

# BUILDING BLOCKS

## Thank you for reading my book, about my food and my life . . . but I am about to change *your* life.

Imagine driving home from work, trying to plan out dinner, and you remember that you have my great-grandmother's tamarind sauce in the fridge. You can use it to drizzle over that piece of fish you planned to grill, or simply dress some glass noodles with some vegetables and some leftover chicken or an egg for a healthy and satisfying meal. The red curry paste you made last Sunday is waiting to be simply put in a pot with coconut milk, protein, and vegetables. Or maybe you don't have any of that prepared yet, but you know that my chili dipping sauce can be whipped up in under five minutes to marinate chicken, and can be used as a dip for raw vegetables while you wait for the grill to warm up. You have options. Your meal will come together almost instantly, leaving you time to focus on the people you love.

When I was four years old, I helped my mother make and sell her special curry pastes at her stall in the market in my hometown of Trang, a city in Southern Thailand halfway between the mountains and the ocean. Before and after school, I would cut turmeric root, carry blocks of shrimp paste, and help prepare the ingredients. At home, I watched Mom make nam jim, punchy and tangy dipping sauces that can elevate the flavor of any protein or vegetable. The recipes for dipping sauces and the curry pastes reflect the bold and complex flavors I grew up with: They're how my family made their living, and they are the building blocks of a Southern Thai meal.

If you didn't grow up with them, what you need to know is that these sauces—and the curry pastes in the next section—can turn a dull weeknight meal into a beautiful and elegant family dinner, or a fast and cheerful spread for unexpected guests. Once you have prepared these dips and sauces and spice blends, they are like an old friend waiting for you in your fridge or freezer, ready to support you whenever you need them.

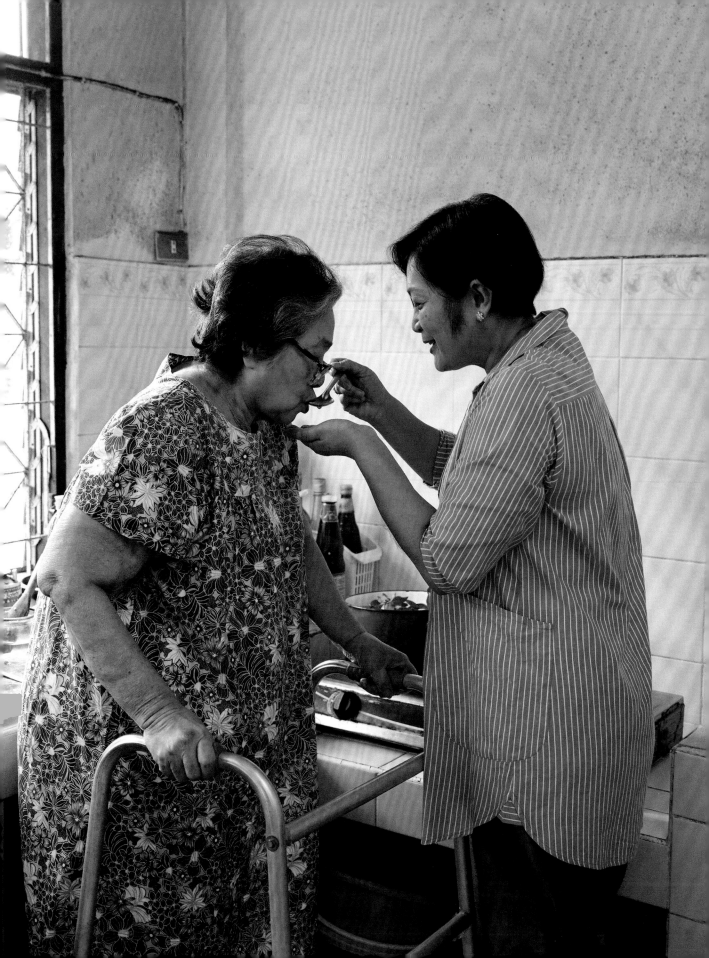

## Nam Jim
### Dipping Sauces

In my cuisine, dipping sauces are as essential as ketchup and mayo in someone else's. Maybe more so, because you don't actually have ketchup at every meal, do you? Sometimes I can't tell here.

Spicy, sour, aromatic, and savory, *nam jim* means "dipping sauce," and variations include Nam Jim Seafood (page 34), Nam Jim Tao Jiew (below, Fermented Bean Sauce) and Nam Jim Jaew (page 38, Charred Aromatic Tamarind Chili Dipping Sauce). We always have at least two sauces on the table, to add flavor and to let everyone create their own experience. The style and number of sauces are based on what is served that day, and if you are eating at home or at a restaurant.

When cooking at home, these sauces can be used in many ways; they are dips, marinades, dressings, and even the base of soup stock. Use them how you want! There is only one rule. Please be sophisticated: Use a little at a time to add or improve flavor. Don't dump it all over your food!

# NAM JIM TAO JIEW
## fermented bean sauce

**MAKES 2 CUPS**

Please don't cry, everything will be okay! Working in my mother's kitchen, I cried a lot, as I chopped, pounded, and minced the freshest of chilies, ginger, and garlic. Making food should inspire you, and using truly fresh ingredients should make you feel something in your heart, even if they make you feel something in your nose and eyes. The Thai fermented soybean paste (tao jiew) in this recipe gives this dipping sauce a salty and umami character, while the chilies, soy sauce, garlic, and sugar balance it. (You can use white miso in place of fermented soybean paste.) In Southern Thailand we serve it with poached fish with a little garlic oil and Chinese celery. You can also pair it with simply cooked chicken or seafood and rice for a crowd-pleasing and easy meal.

5 tablespoons Thai fermented soybean paste (tao jiew) or white miso

¼ cup fresh lime juice or lemon juice (about 2 limes or 1½ lemons)

½ cup plus 1 tablespoon soy sauce

½ cup sugar

1 tablespoon kosher salt

½ cup coarsely chopped peeled fresh ginger (about 3 ounces unpeeled)

½ cup Thai chilies (mix of red and green), roughly chopped (about 25 chilies)

½ cup chopped garlic (about 15 large cloves)

In a food processor or blender, combine the soybean paste, lime juice, soy sauce, sugar, salt, ginger, chilies, and garlic, and blend until uniform in color and just a little chunky. The sauce will keep in an airtight container in the refrigerator for up to 1 month.

# NAM JIM SEAFOOD
## seafood sauce

Seafood sauce is part of Talay Pao culture, the seafood grill stalls you can find all over Thailand. The stalls would serve this spicy sauce of chilies, garlic, lime, and fish sauce with squid, mussels, or whatever was in stock that day. Eating seafood was a special treat because it was expensive, and so for a lot of people, the seafood sauce reminds them of special times, but is versatile enough for every day and any meal. Every family in Southern Thailand has their own seafood sauce and use it for much more than seafood; their own recipes and the different tastes are based on preference. Some families use more garlic, shallot, or chilies to bring out the richness and depth in this savory sauce.

Yes, there are 20 Thai chilies in this recipe, and that is how it should be. It's meant to be hot, and the chilies offer a clean and brilliant heat. I need you to trust me, and try it with the 20 chilies first so you can understand the true nature and beauty of this simple sauce. If the heat is intense for you, use just a little bit—it has a lot of flavor, and you will improve your meal even if you adjust for how much heat you like.

In the South, it is served as a dip with seafood like clams and fried calamari. I encourage you to use it as a dip, marinade, or dressing and serve it as a condiment with any protein because it is so balanced with a sweet heat and citrusy flavors. It turns a basic meal into a flavor adventure. And it can be made in under 10 minutes in a food processor or in a personal smoothie blender. Just don't drink it after.

2 tablespoons packed fresh cilantro leaves

20 red Thai chilies, stemmed

Heaping ⅓ cup garlic cloves, peeled but whole

2 tablespoons packed light brown sugar or palm sugar

5 tablespoons fresh lime juice (about 2½ limes)

2½ tablespoons fish sauce

2 tablespoons water

2 teaspoons kosher salt

In a blender or food processor, combine all the ingredients and pulse until the cilantro, chilies, and garlic are very finely chopped but not pureed. The sauce is best the day it is made, but it will be fresh kept in an airtight container in the refrigerator for up to 1 week.

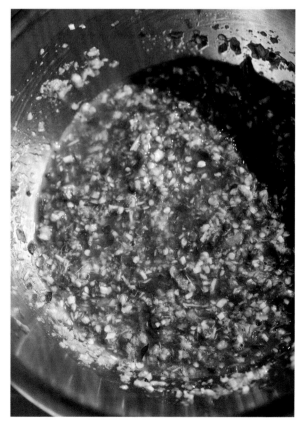

# NAM JIM MAAKAM

## my great-grandma's tamarind sauce

MAKES 1 CUP

This tamarind sauce is like a precious and good olive oil to my family—we would use it as a dip, and it is always on our table. The flavor of this sauce goes in every direction: fruity, sour-sweet-savory-spicy. When you make it, you create a base by cooking palm sugar in soy sauce, then you simmer that with tart tamarind. To finish, you add some raw shallots, chilies, and some more tamarind to keep its fresh flavor.

My great-grandmother would grill fish wrapped in a banana leaf over charcoal and have tamarind sauce on the table to pair with vegetables, relish, and rice. This is a dipping sauce that is always a perfect pairing for fish and seafood on the grill, or you can use it as a dressing for noodles or even salad. Or use it as a flavor base for a soup. Always have this in the fridge; the possibilities for new meals are endless.

2 (70g) discs palm sugar or ½ cup brown sugar

2 tablespoons soy sauce

2 to 3 teaspoons kosher salt

½ cup plus 3 tablespoons tamarind concentrate (see page 22)

½ cup thinly sliced shallot (about 1 large shallot)

5 to 7 Thai chilies, very thinly sliced

1  In a small saucepan, combine the palm sugar and soy sauce and bring to a boil over high heat. Reduce the heat to medium and cook, stirring and scraping the sides and bottom of the pan frequently, until the palm sugar is fully melted (no need to break up the sugar; just be patient and let it dissolve).

2  Stir in the salt and all but 1 tablespoon of the tamarind concentrate and cook on low, stirring frequently, for 3 to 5 minutes to meld the flavors.

3  Remove the pan from the heat, pour the sauce into a small bowl, and let it cool to room temperature. Stir in the shallot and chilies and remaining 1 tablespoon tamarind concentrate. The sauce is freshest kept in an airtight container for up to 1 week.

# NAM PLA WAAN PAK CHEE
## palm sugar & fish sauce relish *with* fried garlic & shallots

**MAKES 1½ CUPS**

When I am frying shallots for this sauce, I am reminded of my home. My mom was always perceived as tough, but her cooking was elegant. As she made this sauce, she was calm, and the shallots changing golden colors were so beautiful; the whole process was like a meditation. This sauce reminds me of times of togetherness, family meals. There are dozens of styles of nam pla waan, a very ancient sauce belonging to Thai cuisine with the base of tamarind sauce, sugar, and fish sauce. In my family, we add fried garlic, fried shallot, and chilies, but my grandmother would add peanuts. This is the base of many Southern Thai salads, and it can be paired with grilled seafood and fish.

¼ cup fish sauce

4 (70g) discs palm sugar
  or 1 cup brown sugar

⅔ cup plus ½ cup
  tamarind concentrate
  (see page 22)

2 to 3 teaspoons
  kosher salt

¼ cup Fried Shallots or
  onion, homemade
  (page 45) or
  store-bought

¼ cup Fried Garlic,
  homemade
  (page 45) or
  store-bought

½ cup vegetable oil

7 dried red chilies

1 In a small saucepan, combine the fish sauce and palm sugar and bring to a boil over high heat. Reduce the heat to medium and cook, stirring frequently, until the mixture is foamy and the palm sugar is fully melted (no need to break up the sugar; just be patient and let it dissolve).

2 Stir in ⅔ cup of the tamarind concentrate and the salt. When the mixture returns to a boil, still over medium heat, stir the mixture every few minutes; it will get foamy, then bubbly, and then syrupy with some bubbles. When the sauce coats the back of a spoon, take it off the heat and pour it into a small bowl and set aside.

3 If you're frying your own shallots and garlic, do that while the sauce cools. (Save the oil from frying the garlic and use it to fry the dried chilies; or if using store-bought, fry the chilies in the vegetable oil listed.)

4 To fry the chilies, line a plate with paper towels and place it within arm's length of the stove. Pour the vegetable oil into a small saucepan and place it over medium heat (or, if you fried your own garlic, reheat the same oil over medium heat after you remove the garlic from the pan). Add the whole dried chilies to the oil and cook just until the chilies sizzle and brighten in color, 1 to 2 minutes. Immediately remove the pan from the heat and stir for 15 to 30 seconds to let them infuse. Use a slotted spoon to transfer the chilies to the paper towels.

5 Once the sauce has cooled completely, stir in the remaining ½ cup tamarind concentrate and the fried shallots and garlic. Crumble the fried dried chilies into the bowl and stir well. The sauce will keep at its freshest refrigerated in an airtight container for up to 1 week.

# NAM JIM JAEW
## charred aromatic tamarind chili dipping sauce

MAKES 1¾ CUPS

In Mexican cuisine, many salsas are started by charring onions, garlic, chilies, and tomatoes before being blended, giving them a deep, smoky flavor that adds complexity to the freshness of the ingredients. This dipping sauce uses a similar technique and will make any average barbecue dish stand out with bright citrus from the lime, sweet and sour tamarind, and heat from dry chili flakes.

I love using tomatoes from my summer garden in this sauce. It's a refreshing dip for grilled or roasted meats, and it can also be used as a wonderful salad dressing. Toasted rice powder (see page 18) acts as a thickener, but it won't be the end of the world if you don't add it.

6 cherry tomatoes, halved

2 red long hot chilies, sliced

5 large garlic cloves, halved

2 large shallots, sliced

2 tablespoons red chili flakes

5 tablespoons fish sauce

⅓ cup plus 2 tablespoons tamarind concentrate (see page 22)

2 to 3 teaspoons kosher salt

1 tablespoon granulated sugar

3 tablespoons fresh lime juice (about 1½ limes)

2 scallions, white and light-green parts only, thinly sliced

2 fresh culantro leaves (see page 17), minced (about 1 tablespoon)

1 tablespoon packed minced fresh cilantro

1 tablespoon Toasted Rice Powder (optional; page 18)

1  In a large dry skillet, spread the cherry tomatoes, chilies, garlic, and shallots in a single layer. Set over medium-high heat and cook, stirring and flipping every couple of minutes, until everything is charred in spots, the shallots are translucent, and the tomatoes blister. Remove from the heat and stir the chili flakes into the vegetables for about 30 seconds, until you don't hear sizzling anymore.

2  Pour the fish sauce over the charred vegetables and use a wooden spoon or spatula to scrape up the browned bits from the bottom of the skillet.

3  Place the vegetable mixture in a mortar and pestle or food processor and grind into a smooth paste, then pour it into a bowl. Stir in the tamarind concentrate, salt, sugar, lime juice, scallions, culantro, and cilantro. The sauce will remain freshest refrigerated in an airtight container for up to 1 week.

4  If you have the toasted rice powder, stir it in just before serving.

# USING A MORTAR AND PESTLE

If you want a good workout and you have time to kill, use the mortar and pestle. I believe that a homemade curry paste made in the blender or food processor is already going to be life-changingly good, but there are those who believe a mortar and pestle is the key to the *very* best curry paste. If you want to try it that way, I'm not going to stop you!

The first thing is that you need a big mortar and pestle; don't use one of the cute little ones you find in nice Western kitchen stores. You need a Thai-style stone mortar; it will be big and heavy. (The lighter clay ones are for Thai salads, not curry pastes.)

When making a curry paste with this tool, you add garlic, shallots, chilies, and salt and pepper first, before you add any hard or large ingredients. Add the garlic, pound it, and once it's mushy, like a paste, add the shallots. When you can't bear it anymore, add the chilies, because why not? You like pain! You decided to do it the old way. Then add the salt. Then when it gets all well combined, add the shrimp paste right away, or the herbs, and so on.

The secret is to smash everything hard, but in control so you don't make a mess. Also, if you are using the mortar and pestle, skip the water in the recipe so you don't splash anything into your eyes. This is the safest way to use a mortar and pestle without hurting yourself or cursing me.

After you embark on this pursuit once, think about all the housewives and moms who have been working all day, who will need to make a quick meal and are thrilled that technology has become accessible! They will make their paste in the food processor.

# NAM JIM WAAN

## sweet chili sauce

**MAKES 1½ CUPS**

This sauce is glossy and beautiful, just like you! When I make it, there is a joy in watching the bright orange and red hue change as the mixture caramelizes and makes a sweet and spicy sauce that can be paired with almost anything. When you try my sweet chili sauce, you will never go back to the oversweetened store-bought version, unless you are lazy, and that is not my problem.

Okay, if you are just *a little bit* lazy, here is a tip: You can use ¾ cup prepared chili-garlic sambal instead of the fresh long chilies and garlic in this recipe.

Red long hot chilies are used a lot because they are brighter, milder, and easier to find, and they are more affordable than Thai chilies.

15 large garlic cloves, peeled but whole

1 cup chopped red long hot chilies (such as cayenne)

1½ cups sugar

1 cup light corn syrup

½ cup distilled white vinegar

2 to 3 tablespoons kosher salt

1  In a food processor, pulse the garlic and chilies until they are very finely chopped.

2  In a medium saucepan, combine the sugar, corn syrup, and ¼ cup water. Bring to a boil over high heat, stirring frequently. Reduce the heat to medium-low and cook, stirring occasionally with a heatproof silicone spatula, until the syrup coats the back of a spoon and is thick enough to hang in droplets on the spatula, about 15 minutes.

3  Stir in the chopped garlic/chili mixture, the vinegar, and salt. Increase the heat to high, bring the mixture to a boil, then reduce the heat back to medium-low. Cook, stirring frequently, for 5 to 7 minutes, then remove the pan from the heat.

4  Pour the sauce into a jar or other container and let it cool completely to room temperature. Don't worry if it looks thin and liquidy at this stage; the sauce will thicken up as it cools. Keep it indefinitely in an airtight container in the refrigerator. If it gets too thick after a long time in the fridge, thin it out with a tablespoon or two of white vinegar before serving.

# PRIK DONG
## chili & vinegar relish

MAKES ABOUT 1½ CUPS

This simple condiment is always on every street stall condiment tray in Southern Thailand; made of chilies soaked in vinegar, it offers a hot sourness to any dish. We call it a relish, but think of it as a quick-pickled chili condiment. To add visual depth, combine different types of red and green chilies, like jalapeño, ghost pepper, or habanero or whatever you have growing in the garden. Prik dong can accompany any noodle or soup to taste, and the vinegar—or chilies themselves—is considered an essential balancing element to salty, sweet, and savory flavors.

1 cup distilled white vinegar

½ cup thinly sliced red long hot chilies or jalapeños (add a few slices of ghost pepper or habanero if you like it extra spicy)

2 to 3 teaspoons kosher salt

Pour the vinegar into a glass jar or other airtight container, add the chilies and salt, and stir well. Let sit at room temperature or in the fridge for at least 1 hour before serving. The condiment will be freshest kept in an airtight container in the refrigerator for up to 1 week.

# PRIK NAM PLA
## fish sauce & chili condiment

MAKES ABOUT 1 CUP

This is an "everything sauce" that can be served with rice, eggs, or vegetables, combining savory, salty fish sauce with chilies, pungent raw garlic, and tart lime. When you go to any restaurant in Thailand, prik nam pla will always be in the condiment tray for you to amp up any dish. You will make this in no time and have it ready to go. Try to find the best-quality fish sauce to make this condiment shine.

¼ cup fish sauce

15 red and green Thai chilies, thinly sliced

½ cup fresh lime or lemon juice (about 4 limes or 3 lemons)

12 large garlic cloves, very thinly sliced

In a jar or other container, mix together the fish sauce, chilies, lime juice, and garlic. The sauce will keep almost indefinitely in an airtight container in the refrigerator.

# FRIED SHALLOTS

Fried shallots and fried garlic are not considered "sauces," but they are used often, and you'll want to keep them around to use in my recipes or anything you eat at home. Fried shallots add a comforting crunch and an exciting aroma to soup, eggs, and stir-fry dishes. Keep the shallot oil, and use it instead of vegetable oil for any savory recipe. Make sure to make double, as you may find yourself snacking on the shallots while you cook.

2 cups thinly sliced shallots, separated into strands

1 tablespoon all-purpose flour or rice flour

1 teaspoon kosher salt, plus more as needed

Vegetable oil, for frying

1  Spread the sliced shallots in a single layer on a clean kitchen towel and let them dry for 1 hour.

2  Transfer the shallots to a medium bowl. Toss with the flour and salt until evenly coated.

3  Line a baking sheet with paper towels. Fill a medium pot with 1 inch of vegetable oil. Place the pot over high heat and toss in one or two strands of shallot. When the shallot starts to sizzle and turn brown, the oil is hot enough.

4  Add a handful of shallots to the hot oil, separating the strands as you drop them. Reduce the heat to medium and fry, stirring frequently, until the shallots are golden brown (they will keep crisping as they dry). Use a slotted spoon to transfer the shallots to the paper towels. Sprinkle the fried shallots with a pinch or two of salt and toss well.

5  Let the shallots cool completely, then store them in an airtight container indefinitely at room temperature. If they lose their crispness, reheat them in a 325°F oven for a couple of minutes to re-crisp them.

# FRIED GARLIC & GARLIC OIL

Fried garlic (you can choose either slices or little chopped garlic bits) give you great flavor and crisp texture. We love to use it with noodles. And the oil you fried it in is also delicious for finishing dishes at the table.

½ cup vegetable oil

7 large garlic cloves, very thinly sliced, or ¼ cup finely chopped garlic (about 10 cloves)

Line a plate with paper towels and place it within arm's reach of the stove. Pour the vegetable oil into a small saucepan and place it over medium heat. Add the garlic and cook. The garlic will sizzle and eventually change color; this will take 2 to 5 minutes, depending on how small the garlic is cut. Stir frequently. When most of the slices are just light golden brown, turn off the heat and stir the garlic vigorously until all the bits are evenly browned. Be careful because it can burn easily; you don't want it to turn dark brown. Use a slotted spoon to transfer the garlic to the paper towels. Use the fried garlic immediately or store in an airtight container. Reserve the garlic oil in a small jar in the fridge for future use. Both will keep a long time, but you will eat them before they go stale.

## Prik Kaeng
### Curry Pastes and
### Dry Spice Blends

To this day, I still think my mom's curry paste is the best. She sourced the freshest spices and herbs and used seasonal ingredients, but just as important, she had the power to listen to the ingredients; if the color of lime leaf was dull or the shrimp paste was not aged enough, she would adjust the ingredients to find the ideal balance of flavor. Her customers knew that no matter what the season, my mother would provide an outstanding product. I have committed my life to doing the same with my food.

My homemade curry pastes may be unlike anything you've tasted. They are fresh and herbaceous and jump off the palate to tell a story of hard work and love. Because you will make these curry pastes for the people you love. The hard work part—well, that's up to you.

While I grew up getting a workout by pounding the pastes in a large mortar and pestle, I eventually switched to using a very large grinder. In this era, you don't need to use a mortar and pestle, but if you want to, you can (see Using a Mortar and Pestle (see the sidebar on page 39). Either method you choose will still create something delicious that preserves the integrity of the ingredients and the flavors, and there is no trade-off in taste. These days, most people have access to modern technology and grind their pastes in a machine. Thailand is about convenience, and people buy their curry pastes from the market or use a food processor at home!

If most of your experience with Thai food is in restaurants in America, you probably know curries by their color, with your choice of protein mixed in. The way I was taught to make curry is not defined by colors; it is defined by the main ingredients or flavors, such as pepper curry, sour curry, and coconut milk curry, which are all specific to Southern Thailand. The curry paste I use most often in my restaurant, Kalaya House Curry Paste (page 55), is a yellow curry paste, but when I use it in dishes, it's with an intentional purpose and with specific pairings of ingredients.

That said, in your home, you may use the curry pastes that follow in ways that may surprise you. The recipes will make fairly large batches, enough for several meals. You may divide the recipes into smaller quantities, or you can make the whole thing and think about the easy and quick meals you will be making in the future. Just pack it into $\frac{1}{2}$-cup portions in an airtight container and keep it in the freezer—it keeps almost forever in the freezer, or at least a few months. Most home cooks have not tried fresh curry paste before. I assure you, it brings out the best in home-cooked Thai food.

# WAYS TO USE CURRY PASTE
## that's not for a curry (or for a lazy curry)

With all the flavor you create in these curry pastes, you should think of them as bases for all kinds of incredible meals. Of course, if you are lazy (it's okay, I give you permission to be lazy), you can skip any of the recipes I have and do a Lazy Curry: Just add some curry paste to a can or two of coconut milk, simmer it to create a sauce, season with salt, fish sauce, and sugar, then add vegetables or protein, and you have a super-simple curry. Or keep it on hand and do any of the following:

1 Add a few spoonfuls to amp up the flavor of an easy fried rice.

2 Mix with oil and use as you would a chili oil or chili crisp.

3 Add it to a chicken or vegetable soup. Pumpkin would be delicious! (When you are sick, the spices will open up your sinuses! Allergy season? No problem!)

4 Mix curry paste with oil to use as a marinade before roasting or grilling meats or vegetables.

5 Stir a bit into mayonnaise for curry paste aioli, to use on sandwiches or to dip French fries into.

6 Mix with coconut milk and oil for a salad dressing.

7 Mix a spoonful and very thinly sliced makrut lime leaf into ground meat to make Thai style patties or meatballs.

8 Stir a spoonful into beaten eggs and scramble them or make an omelet and enjoy it with rice.

9 Stir a teaspoon to a tablespoon into a box of corn bread mix or scone mix.

# GAENG SOM
## sour curry paste

Sour curry paste's flavor profile is like the Southern Thai people: punchy, direct, and simple. This is an everyday paste—really more a smooth puree—of just chilies, garlic, and shallots that my mom would make after a long day of working in the market; it doesn't have lemongrass, herbs, or other flavors that you might think of when you think of "curry paste." I told you it was simple! But when combined with fish and vegetables and lime juice and tamarind, it makes the Southern Thai classic called sour curry (such as Sour Curry with Shrimp and Pineapple, page 118). If you like garlic, shallots, and especially chilies, this is a great paste to keep on hand for "off menu" uses in your home, like starting a stir-fry or finishing something with a big kick of flavor.

¾ cup roughly chopped red Thai chilies or other small red chilies (about 36 chilies)

8 large garlic cloves, roughly chopped

⅔ cup sliced shallots (about 3 large)

1½ to 2 tablespoons kosher salt

⅓ cup water

In a blender (in this case, really use a blender, not a food processor), combine all the ingredients and process until smooth, scraping down the sides as needed. Refrigerate for up to 3 days or freeze any leftover paste in a zip-top bag or other airtight container for up to 3 months.

# GAENG KUA PRIG
## pepper curry paste

This is a very spicy curry paste with no mercy—using fresh and dried chilies, the brightness of lemongrass, and the heat of white pepper and black pepper makes it unique and bold. When you use this in a curry, it will make you sweat, but you will want to keep eating more. This is a highly concentrated curry paste.

8 stalks fresh lemongrass, tender white part only (see page 17), very finely chopped (about ½ cup)

½ cup red chili flakes

3 tablespoons freshly ground black pepper

3 tablespoons ground white pepper

½ cup roughly chopped fresh red Thai chilies (about 25 chilies)

¼ cup chopped peeled fresh turmeric

2 tablespoons chopped peeled galangal, fresh or thawed if frozen

2 large shallots, thinly sliced (about ½ cup)

8 large garlic cloves, roughly chopped

2 tablespoons packed thinly sliced makrut lime leaves

1½ to 2 tablespoons kosher salt

1 cup water

In a food processor, combine all the ingredients and process until very smooth. You can refrigerate the paste for up to 1 week or freeze any leftover paste in a zip-top bag or other airtight container for up to 3 months.

# GAENG DANG

## red curry paste

Red curry is not supposed to be too spicy; it should have a bright mellow flavor that pairs well with sweet flavors, like pineapple. The ingredients galangal, paprika, lemongrass, and black pepper in this recipe are well-balanced. I love using the paste for a quick dry curry like Pad Prik King Hed (page 135, Dry Red Curry with Pan-Fried Tofu and Mushrooms), and Chuchee Hoi Shell (page 139, Dinner Party Seared Scallops and Crabmeat in Yellow Curry Sauce) or Panang Gai (page 121, Chicken Panang Curry) that you can make in the wok. The meal comes together so quickly with just a bit of coconut milk; but the longer you cook your curry sauce, the more the balanced, complex flavor will really shine.

And while the use of paprika may surprise you, we use it a lot in South and Central Thailand. Paprika plays a major part in the rich color and mild flavors, without any additives or dyes.

½ cup sweet paprika

½ cup red chili flakes

½ cup packed minced fresh lemongrass (see page 17), tender white part only (about 8 stalks)

10 large garlic cloves, roughly chopped (about ½ cup)

3 large shallots, sliced (about ⅔ cup)

3 tablespoons finely chopped peeled galangal, fresh or thawed if frozen

5 makrut lime leaves, thinly sliced (1 packed tablespoon)

¼ cup roughly chopped fresh cilantro roots and/or stems

3 tablespoons freshly ground black pepper

1 tablespoon ground white pepper

1½ to 2 tablespoons kosher salt

1¼ cups water

In a blender or food processor, combine the paprika, chili flakes, lemongrass, garlic, shallots, galangal, lime leaves, cilantro roots, black pepper, white pepper, salt, and water, and stir to distribute everything evenly, then process until smooth. You can store it in the fridge for up to 1 week, then freeze any leftover paste in a zip-top bag or other airtight container for up to 3 months.

# GAENG KIEW WAAN

## green curry paste

**MAKES 5 CUPS**

My mom would never let me write down her recipes; she would tell me and I would have to remember everything. Then I would run to the Chinese pharmacy and tell my list. (Chinese pharmacies are the same as a spice store, and where my mom got a lot of herbs for her business.) When helping my mom with this paste at ten years old, I would run into the store, grab the spices, run home to toast it, and feel excited to get my work done. I knew I couldn't take a shortcut or my mom would know. I can still remember her saying "Not enough! Keep going!" reminding me that I needed to pound the spice with the mortar and pestle.

This paste is the color of jungle camouflage. It is refreshing, creamy, and sweet to go with the chilies and all those spices I used to pound—cumin and coriander, and black and white pepper. It is perfect with seafood or also braised beef like osso buco (see page 127). When you think about green curry paste as a type of pesto, the pairing options become endless. Make a green curry pasta, stir-fry seafood with it, or add it to a soup with pumpkin.

2 tablespoons ground cumin, preferably ground from freshly toasted seeds (see page 18)

1 tablespoon ground black pepper

3 tablespoons ground white pepper

1½ to 2 tablespoons kosher salt

½ cup water

½ cup minced fresh lemongrass (see page 17), tender white part only (about 8 stalks)

5 makrut lime leaves, torn

2 cups chopped green Thai chilies

¼ cup finely chopped peeled galangal, fresh or thawed if frozen

⅔ cup packed chopped fresh cilantro leaves and tender stems

⅔ cup packed fresh basil leaves, chopped

8 large garlic cloves, roughly chopped (about ⅓ cup)

2 large shallots, roughly chopped (½ cup packed)

3 tablespoons ground coriander, preferably ground from freshly toasted seeds (see page 18)

In a blender or food processor, combine all the ingredients, stir to distribute everything evenly, then process until smooth. You can refrigerate the paste for up to 3 days, then freeze any leftover paste in a zip-top bag or other airtight container for up to 3 months.

# KALAYA HOUSE CURRY PASTE

**MAKES ABOUT 5 CUPS**

My mom's fresh curry paste is unlike anything you've had before. This is a yellow curry paste, and the house curry paste that we use at the restaurant, meaning we use it for lots of different things, including our chicken curry, the most beloved dish on our menu. But I also call it the house curry paste because we also used to make about 110 pounds of this every day at my mom's stall—so it was always in our house!

The yellow color comes from turmeric, which gives it a wonderful earthiness. Chili peppers and the ratio of white and black pepper add heat and sharpness, while the galangal, lime leaf, and lemongrass add a bright citrus flavor.

¼ cup thinly sliced fresh lemongrass (see page 17), tender white parts only (about 3 thick stalks)

¼ cup finely chopped peeled galangal, fresh or thawed if frozen

6 tablespoons finely chopped peeled fresh turmeric

½ cup plus 2 tablespoons red chili flakes

6 tablespoons sweet paprika

20 red Thai chilies, chopped

¼ cup freshly ground black pepper

¼ cup ground white pepper

½ cup large garlic cloves, chopped

1 tablespoon ground turmeric

¾ cup plus 2 tablespoons thinly sliced shallots

10 makrut lime leaves, sliced

1½ cups water

In a blender or food processor, combine all the ingredients, stir to distribute everything evenly, then process until smooth. You can refrigerate this for up to 1 week, then freeze any leftover paste in a zip-top bag or other airtight container for up to 3 months.

# TURMERIC PASTE

**MAKES ABOUT 2 CUPS**

This is another special recipe from my mother's kitchen. Turmeric paste is something we always have in the kitchen; it's simple and makes everything taste better. It's not really a curry paste, you can't make a curry with it, but you can make amazing chicken with it—my mom would marinate any and every protein with it from fish to pork. You can use it like a spice rub—just smear it on the meat, or even a scored whole fish, and sauté it a few minutes later. We use this paste in Pla Kamin (page 163, Turmeric Fish) and Khao Pad Kamin (page 236, Turmeric Fried Rice). The turmeric adds a mellow gingery flavor and the pepper adds heat. The color of this paste is soothing, like the sun shining down on my garden. The turmeric powder in America is different from that in Southern Thailand, so combining fresh turmeric root and turmeric powder is essential to create the correct flavor profile.

1 cup roughly chopped peeled fresh turmeric (from about 5 ounces)

2 to 3 teaspoons kosher salt

1¼ cups garlic cloves, peeled but whole

½ cup fresh ground black pepper

¼ cup ground white pepper

2 tablespoons ground turmeric

In a blender or food processor, combine all the ingredients, stir to distribute everything evenly, then process until as smooth as possible. (The smoothness depends on how moist your fresh turmeric is; it's okay if it comes out a little chunky in the end.) Refrigerate for up to 1 week, then freeze any leftover paste in a zip-top bag or other airtight container for up to 3 months.

## Spice Blends
### Kruang Tase

Are you an overachiever? Then make your own dry spice blends. You can use them in recipes like Spicy Celebration Goat Curry (page 132, Kang Pae) and Morning Market Chicken Biryani (page 69, Khao Mok Ghai). When you make your own spice blends, the flavor is warm, fragrant, and it feels more true to my hometown, where we are constantly grinding and toasting our spices fresh. There is something so thrilling about going to the fresh spice shop in Trang, between the beautiful earthy colors to the powerful fragrance taking you back to all the spice routes that changed the way we cook forever. Try to find organic spices when you can, and avoid ground spices with lots of fillers. You will know when you open the jar whether it smells vibrant or stale. It's a fun project, and just by doing it, you will get an A+.

# NOK'S KAREE POWDER

**MAKES ABOUT ½ CUP**

My karee powder is a fresh and bold recipe from Trang. We use this for the glaze in our Gai Yaang Kamin (page 204, Grilled Turmeric Chicken) and our Goong Phao and Pla Meuk Yaang (page 207, Grilled Prawns and Three-Minute Grilled Squid), as well as one of our favorites, Poo Pad Pong Karee (page 168, Stir-Fried Crab in Curry Powder Sauce). It is a type of curry powder that is mellow and bright at the same time, and you won't find this easily in the United States. You'll smile while you are making it because of its burnished golden color and beautiful fragrance.

So much American curry powder is made with fillers or mixed from dull, stale old spices, but here, you will sense the sharpness from the black and white pepper, and that floral bite of the ground ginger. Just make sure you're starting with spices that are still fresh enough to make your eyes open up when you breathe them in.

28 green cardamom pods

1 tablespoon yellow mustard seeds

2 tablespoons coriander seeds

2 tablespoons ground turmeric

1 tablespoon sweet paprika

1 tablespoon ground ginger

1 teaspoon freshly ground black pepper

1 teaspoon ground white pepper

Put the cardamom pods in a spice grinder and process to a fine powder, then add the mustard seeds, coriander, turmeric, paprika, ginger, black pepper, and white pepper, and grind again until powdery. Keep in an airtight container in the pantry for up to 3 months.

# FIVE-SPICE POWDER

**MAKES ABOUT ⅓ CUP**

Sure, you can get five-spice powder in the grocery store, but that is not magical or inspiring! When you make your own five-spice blend, there is more flavor, there is more activation of your senses and your heart when you smell the anise and the cinnamon and the fennel grinding and toasting together. You are a strong person for making the effort, and you will taste the difference. Toasting these spices brings out a warm, earthy, sharp flavor. You can use this five-spice powder for Moo Hong (page 228, Braised Pork Belly) and gift it to your friends.

8 star anise pods

1 tablespoon whole cloves

1 tablespoon Sichuan peppercorns

2 tablespoons fennel seeds

3 tablespoons ground cinnamon

1   Put the star anise pods in a spice grinder and process to a coarse powder. Add the cloves, peppercorns, fennel seeds, and cinnamon and grind again to a fine powder.

2   Scrape the ground spices into a dry medium skillet, set over medium heat, and toast just until fragrant. Immediately transfer to a container that can be closed airtight. Let cool completely, cover, and store in the pantry for about 1 month (any longer and the spice blend will lose its fragrance).

# KRUANG RAH SPICE

**MAKES ¾ CUP**

This aromatic, warming spice blend is not unlike garam masala in Indian cooking. It's used in our Kang Pae (page 132, Spicy Celebration Goat Curry) and Kua Gling Nua (page 113, Toasted Beef Curry). The spice has an earthy depth because of the toasting. Remember when you are toasting spices, the cumin should dance a little. It's so fun to watch the spices take on a new aroma and realize their potential. This is the perfect spice blend for game or red meat.

2 tablespoons cumin seeds

¼ cup coriander seeds

28 green cardamom pods

2 teaspoons ground cinnamon

2 teaspoons ground nutmeg

¼ cup freshly ground black pepper

2 tablespoons ground white pepper

1   In a small dry skillet, working with one spice at a time, toast the cumin, coriander, and cardamom over medium heat until they are fragrant and darker in color, 2 to 3 minutes each. Place the toasted spices in separate small bowls.

2   Place the cinnamon and nutmeg in the skillet, set over medium heat for 30 seconds, then turn off the heat and stir to toast and warm up the spices.

3   Once the cardamom and coriander seeds are cooled slightly, put them in a spice grinder or mortar. Grind until powdery, then add the cumin, cinnamon, and nutmeg and grind again to a powder. Pour the ground spices into an airtight container and stir in the black and white pepper. Seal the container and store it in the pantry. The spice blend will keep its best flavor for up to 3 months.

# BREAKFAST IN TRANG

**In America, we are running with our coffee.
We are shoveling pastries into our mouths
without thinking, and we are not appreciating
the stillness and beauty of the morning.**

In Trang, my home province, we don't rush. We celebrate the
nowness of every day and every morning.

It's that first sip of strong filtered robusta coffee, while holding
a newspaper as the sunlight shines into an open-air all-day café.
The laminate table starts out empty as you read the day's news
events and chat about it with your cousin and fellow diners. Slowly,
all sorts of small dishes start appearing: a beautiful shumai, some
roasted pork, poached eggs, congee, noodles, steamed buns, and
roti, and there is barely an inch of room to spare. It's our take on
dim sum, and it's absolutely joyful.

Trang breakfast evolved during the 1800s, when Chinese
migrant workers on the rubber plantations had to rise extremely
early to tap the trees. For many of these workers, these new jobs
meant there was new access to produce, and while the work was
very hard and often under inhumane conditions, they also brought
their food traditions and influenced Trang cuisine. While waiting
for the trees to produce, they'd go have a full breakfast, until they
went back to work.

But Trang breakfast doesn't exactly stop at breakfast time. The
cafés today are open all day. Many of the recipes in this chapter can
be served all day, for dinner, or as a snack.

I wanted to start this book first with the building blocks of my
cuisine—the sauces and curry pastes—and then these recipes,
because they are an introduction to the culture of the place I grew
up in. But whether you make these recipes first or go searching
elsewhere in the book to start cooking, I encourage you to wake up
in the morning with your strong coffee and plan a comforting meal
to enjoy the little special things in life.

# KANOM JEEN
## rice noodles *with* coconut fish curry

SERVES 4

I love bold art, and for me, the rice noodles in this recipe are like a canvas ready to paint.

Every market in Thailand has a kanom jeen stall, and it's a buildable dish where a curry sauce and fresh vegetables come together in a rainbow of texture and color alongside nests of tender rice noodles. There is the crunch from the cucumbers, pineapple, raw cabbage, sator beans, and long beans, and a delicate, bright, and creamy flavor from the coconut and fish. Kanom jeen has so much depth, and you can add as much or little crunchy vegetables as you like depending on your tastes. This is a family-friendly, kid-friendly dish that everyone will love. It's extremely nourishing and comforting anytime, but when we eat it for breakfast, we know it will give you the energy to work hard on the farm, or the laptop, all day.

I encourage you to be adventurous with the curry sauce and raw vegetables even if you don't have rice noodles. Maybe serve them over angel hair pasta or even gnocchi, and enjoy Nok's gnocchi!

### COCONUT FISH CURRY

1 pound mackerel fillets or other rich fish, skinned and cut into large chunks

2 (13.5-ounce) cans coconut milk (3½ cups)

½ cup Kalaya House Curry Paste (page 55)

1 tablespoon shrimp paste

1 lemongrass stalk, smashed and tied in a knot

2 tablespoons Ground Dried Shrimp (page 137)

1 tablespoon kosher salt

½ tablespoon light brown sugar

3 makrut lime leaves, torn

### FOR SERVING

8 to 12 ounces fresh rice vermicelli noodles or 4 to 6 ounces dried

Lots of shredded or thinly sliced raw vegetables, such as carrots, cabbage, cucumber, long beans, etc.

4 hard-boiled eggs, halved or cut into wedges

Seasonings: Fish sauce, soy sauce, kosher salt, red chili flakes

4 lime wedges, for squeezing

1   **Make the coconut fish curry:** In a medium saucepan, combine the fish with enough water to fully submerge it. Bring to a boil over high heat. Reduce to a simmer and cook for a couple of minutes, just until you can easily flake it with a fork. Use a slotted spoon to transfer the fish to a blender, reserving the cooking liquid in the pan.

2   Add 1 cup of the coconut milk and 1 cup of the fish cooking liquid to the blender with the fish. Process until smooth.

3   In a medium saucepan, bring 2 cups of the coconut milk to a boil over high heat. Add the pureed fish mixture, curry paste, shrimp paste, lemongrass, ground dried shrimp, salt, and brown sugar. Bring to a boil, using a wooden spoon to break up the shrimp paste. Then reduce the heat to medium-low and simmer for 5 minutes, stirring occasionally.

4   Stir in the remaining ½ cup coconut milk and the makrut lime leaves, cook for a minute or two, and remove the pan from the heat.

5   **To serve:** Cook the vermicelli noodles according to the package directions. Drain the noodles and keep them long, like spaghetti, as the noodles symbolize prosperity.

6   Divide the noodles among four bowls. Spoon the curry over the noodles to your preference, top with lots of raw vegetables and the hard-boiled eggs, and serve with the suggested seasonings and lime wedges for squeezing.

# KHAO TOM PLA

## rice soup *with* fish & shrimp

SERVES 4

There is something so comforting about rice soup. This dish is so easy to make, especially if you have leftover cooked rice, and the perfect way to settle an empty stomach between the calming ginger, chicken broth, mild tender fish and shrimp, soft rice, and silky poached eggs. The famous soup places in Southern Thailand really focus on the quality of the broth, and have passed their recipe down for generations. In your house, you may use a good-quality store-bought chicken broth, and while we eat this for breakfast, you can find your own tradition and make this any time you want. This is a family-friendly dish that everyone will love (but it can also cure a hangover).

1 pound red snapper, monkfish, halibut, or swordfish fillets, skinned

4 cups Chicken Broth (page 146, Nam Soup Gai) or store-bought

1½ cups jasmine rice

1 tablespoon kosher salt, or to taste

4 jumbo shrimp, peeled and deveined, tails removed

**FOR SERVING**

Garlic Oil (page 45)

Thinly sliced scallions

Chopped fresh cilantro

4 soft-poached eggs

2 tablespoons thinly sliced peeled fresh ginger

1 stalk Chinese celery, or 1 small regular celery stalk with leaves, very thinly sliced

Ground white pepper

Soy sauce

Chili and Vinegar Relish (page 42, Prik Dong)

1  Slice the fish on an angle into 4-inch-long strips.

2  In a medium saucepan, combine the chicken broth and rice and bring to a boil over medium-high heat. Cook, stirring occasionally, until the rice grains are soft but intact, 7 to 10 minutes. Stir in the salt; if your broth is salty to begin with, just add a little and taste first. Drain the rice in a fine-mesh sieve set over a heatproof bowl, reserving the broth. Divide the rice among four bowls.

3  Return the cooking liquid to the saucepan and set over medium-low heat. Add the fish and shrimp and cook just until the fish and shrimp are firm and opaque, about 3 minutes.

4  **To serve:** Use a slotted spoon to divide the fish and shrimp equally among the individual bowls. Ladle the broth over top, drizzle each bowl with a little garlic oil, and sprinkle with scallions and cilantro. Add a poached egg to each bowl. Top with the fresh ginger and celery and a pinch of white pepper. Serve with soy sauce and prik dong for extra seasoning.

# KHAO MOK CHAI
## morning market chicken biryani

Morning Market Chicken Biryani is Southern comfort. Thai biryani was adapted to Thailand by generations of Indian and Pakistani immigrants who immigrated to Southern Thailand and used the ingredients and cooking equipment available. In khao mok gai, the meat is tender, the rice is perfectly steamed, it's aromatic with spices, and it's never too dry. And it's paired with a sauce that includes nam jim waan (sweet chili sauce) and nam jim seafood (seafood sauce) and is distinctly Thai.

You might think a traditional biryani is filled with many steps, but this is a true one-pot meal meant to be shared with friends. You don't need an oven, and the overnight marination of the chicken may be the only step to consider before you dive into making it. That's the way my mom used to do it, and you should, too.

I think of my mom making this at home for a celebration, or the local vendors stirring a big pot of fragrant, sweetly spiced rice with braised chicken, in their open-air stall. The color is a beautiful earthy gold, and gold is a lucky and celebratory color. My favorite stall belonged to a friend of my mom's. We could pick what part of the chicken we wanted (and I would always choose the thigh). The warming comfort from the cinnamon and garam masala is unforgettable, and while it can be a dish for sharing at home, it can also call for celebration.

## CHICKEN

1 cup whole-milk yogurt

3 tablespoons ground turmeric

1½ to 2 tablespoons kosher salt

1 tablespoon freshly ground black pepper

1 tablespoon ground white pepper

2 pounds bone-in, skin-on chicken thighs and drumsticks

7 tablespoons salted butter

2 cups Chicken Broth (page 146, Nam Soup Gai) or store-bought

## RICE

2½ cups jasmine rice

10 large garlic cloves

3 ounces fresh ginger, peeled and chopped (about ½ cup)

1 medium sweet yellow onion, diced (about 1½ cups)

5 star anise pods

20 whole cloves

9 cardamom pods

2 tablespoons Nok's Karee Powder (page 56) or store-bought curry powder

2 cups Chicken Broth (page 146, Nam Soup Gai) or store-bought

1 tablespoon light brown sugar

½ teaspoon freshly ground black pepper

½ teaspoon ground white pepper

3 tablespoons fish sauce

## SAUCE

½ cup Sweet Chili Sauce (page 41, Nam Jim Waan) or store-bought

½ cup Seafood Sauce (page 34, Nam Jim Seafood)

2 tablespoons distilled white vinegar

2 tablespoons finely chopped fresh mint

2 tablespoons finely chopped fresh cilantro

## FOR SERVING

Leaves from 1 bunch fresh cilantro, chopped

Fried Shallots (page 45)

*recipe continues*

1  **Prepare the chicken:** In a large bowl, whisk together the yogurt, turmeric, salt, black pepper, and white pepper. Add the chicken and toss to coat in the yogurt mixture, cover, and refrigerate overnight.

2  In a Dutch oven or other large pot, melt the butter over high heat. Add the marinated chicken and scrape in all the marinade from the bowl. Cook for 5 minutes, turn the chicken, and pour in the chicken broth, using a wooden spatula to scrape up the browned bits from the bottom of the pot. Bring to a boil, reduce the heat to medium-low, and cook uncovered until the chicken registers 165°F on an instant-read thermometer, 20 to 25 minutes.

3  **Meanwhile, make the rice:** Rinse the rice thoroughly under cool running water and drain well.

4  In a food processor, combine the garlic, ginger, and onion and grind until very finely chopped.

5  When the chicken is cooked, use tongs to transfer it to a plate and pour the cooking broth into a heatproof bowl.

6  Return the pot to high heat and add the garlic/ginger/onion mixture, the star anise, cloves, cardamom, and karee powder. Cook for 30 seconds to 1 minute, until fragrant, then add the rice and use the spatula to scrape the bottom of the pot. Cook, stirring, for 1 to 2 minutes, then pour in the cooking broth and 1¼ cups water. Add the brown sugar, black pepper, white pepper, and fish sauce. Cover the pot and cook over medium heat for 5 minutes. Give it a good stir, scraping up any browned bits from the bottom of the pot. Cover and cook for another 3 minutes.

7  Stir well, spread out the rice evenly, and arrange the chicken on top. Cover the pot, reduce the heat to low, and cook until the rice is tender and has absorbed all the liquid, 10 to 12 minutes.

8  **Make the sauce:** In a small bowl, mix together the sweet chili sauce, seafood sauce, vinegar, mint, and cilantro.

9  **To serve:** Top the chicken biryani with the cilantro and fried shallots. Serve with the sauce.

# THIS IS TRANG

I grew up in a village called Yan Ta Khao, near Trang, the capital city in a province also named Trang in Southern Thailand, which serves as the gateway to the Thai Islands. A province of more than 600,000 people, Trang sits along the Andaman coast and features beaches as famously beautiful as those in Phuket and Krabi, without being crowded or overwhelmed by tourism. It is a city that many people pass through but rarely stop to explore, despite our aquamarine ocean, white sand, rain forests, caves, and mountains. But throughout Thailand, Trang is known for its exceptional food, kind people, and a unique blend of Chinese, Thai, and Islamic cultures that was shaped by its importance as a port city and rubber-growing region.

In Trang, food is the heart of everything we do, from family meals and celebrations to shopping at the open-air market in the center of the city. Ordinary people wake up around 4 a.m. to go to the market before work, and by that time dozens of food-stall vendors have been up since 2 a.m. preparing their specialties—including a fried dough snack known as pa tong goh, fried chicken in shallot oil, fried turmeric fish, massaman curry, and roasted sweet pork belly. Every aisle you walk down in the market is exhilarating, with colorful stacks of local fruit such as rambutan, durian, and longan. Here is fresh coconut being pressed into milk, there seafood caught only hours before, and over there, whole pigs being marinated and roasted—and all of that before breakfast even begins.

We joke that in Trang, we eat more than in any other province in Thailand. Some people claim to eat nine small meals a day because the food is so diverse and delicious. We have halal restaurants that serve biryani, seafood restaurants that serve fish freshly caught off nearby docks, and outstanding vegetarian cuisine that is celebrated every October in a ten-day-long vegetarian festival known as Cin Jay. The festival features "jay" food—cuisine that Westerners would consider vegan and also includes no garlic, onion, scallions, or cilantro. Our vegetarian food is balanced and cleansing (but the truth is there also might be a little MSG to extend those delicious flavors . . . and when you are on any kind of cleanse, everything tastes even better afterward!). My favorite festival dishes are red curry with mushrooms, Thai vegetable stew, and fermented vegetable stew.

Whether rich or poor, we would always share our food with family and friends. In elementary school, I had a friend who did not even own shoes, yet her family had coconut trees on their land. They would make coconut oil by simmering coconut cream on very low heat, allowing the cream and oil to separate. She would bring in foraged mushrooms sautéed in the coconut oil to share with me. I remember the purity and nuttiness of the coconut oil and fresh mushrooms to this day.

# KHAO MUN GAI
## chicken & rice

SERVES 4 TO 6

Think about your favorite "plain" pizza. What makes one pizza better than another? It's the crust, the sauce, the cheese. There can be so much variation in all three of those things. It's the same nuance in khao mun gai: It looks basic, just boiled chicken and rice with some dips. But it's one of Thailand's all-time favorite dishes, and a good one features the tenderness of the chicken (and the silkiness of boiled chicken skin), the bite of the rice cooked in the garlic-ginger broth, and the balance of a spicy soy sauce dip.

I go to different chicken and rice stalls all over Thailand, but the best one is in Trang; a couple from my village own the stall, and they always find the best chicken. For this recipe, use the best-quality chicken you can find and make sure you cook the rice so it's not mushy.

If you don't want to see the whole chicken, fine. Get the skinless, boneless, soulless chicken. You can make good khao mun gai with it, but it won't be at its best. Trust me, skin on is the right way to eat the chicken. But look, even if you are not in the Khao Mun Gai World Championship, you will still be eating something delicious.

### CHICKEN AND STOCK
1 whole chicken (4 pounds), cut in half lengthwise
8 large garlic cloves, smashed and peeled
2 ounces fresh ginger, peeled and thinly sliced
Stems from 1 bunch cilantro

### RICE
3 tablespoons minced garlic
⅓ cup canola or vegetable oil
3 ounces fresh ginger, peeled and finely chopped
2 tablespoons salted butter
2 cups jasmine rice, rinsed well under cool running water, and drained
1½ to 2 tablespoons kosher salt
2 teaspoons light brown sugar

### SAUCE
2 tablespoons light brown sugar
1 teaspoon to ½ tablespoon kosher salt
Pinch of ground white pepper
2 tablespoons soy sauce
½ tablespoon sesame oil

### FOR SERVING
¼ cup Thai black soy sauce
2 tablespoons finely chopped Thai chilies
Fermented Bean Sauce (page 33, Nam Jim Tao Jiew)
Sweet Chili Sauce (page 41, Nam Jim Waan)
Sliced cucumbers
Roughly chopped fresh cilantro

1  Cook the chicken and make the stock: Put the chicken in a large stockpot, along with the garlic, ginger, and cilantro stems. Pour in enough cold water to cover the chicken by 2 or 3 inches and set the pot over high heat. When the water begins to boil, reduce the heat to medium and simmer for about 30 minutes, or until the chicken registers 165°F on an instant thermometer in the thickest piece of the meat. Use tongs to transfer the chicken to a cutting board, reserving the stock in the pot.

*recipe continues*

73

2  **Make the rice:** In a medium saucepan, combine the garlic and oil and set over medium heat. When you hear the garlic sizzling, stir it with a wooden spoon and keep cooking, stirring frequently, until it is golden brown, about 3 minutes. Add the ginger and butter and cook, stirring frequently, until the garlic and ginger reach a rich brown color, another 2 to 3 minutes.

3  Stir in the rinsed rice, increase the heat to medium-high, and sauté it with the aromatics, stirring, until the rice is dry, aromatic, and you can see about half of it turn opaque white, about 5 minutes. Carefully add 3¾ cups of the reserved chicken stock, as it will boil and steam at the first splash. (I suggest using a ladle to keep your hand away from the steam.) Add the salt and brown sugar. As soon as the stock bubbles around the edges of the pan, cover, reduce the heat to medium-low, and cook, stirring once halfway through, until the liquid has been absorbed and the rice is tender, about 15 minutes.

4  **Make the sauce:** In a small saucepan, combine 1½ cups of the reserved chicken stock with the brown sugar, salt, white pepper, soy sauce, and sesame oil. Bring to a boil over high heat, then turn off the heat.

5  Remove the bones from the cooked chicken, but keep the skin on. Using the side of your biggest knife, smash the chicken to flatten it a bit. Then slice it and place it on a high-sided plate or platter. Pour the sauce over the top.

6  **To serve:** In a small ramekin, mix together the black soy sauce and Thai chilies. Serve the chicken and rice with the sauces, cucumber slices, cilantro, and small bowls of the remaining warm chicken stock seasoned with a little salt.

# SAKOO SAI MOO
## pork-stuffed tapioca pearls

Do you need a fun rainy-day project for your kids instead of Play-Doh that will get stuck to the carpet? You can play "Auntie Nok's Market Stall" and have the little ones help you make this savory snack for hours of fun.

Many tastes and flavors come together for this treasured market snack, with a crunchy, meaty, sweet-savory filling of pork, peanuts, and herbs stuffed inside a chewy ball of tapioca dough. The filling is highly seasoned because the tapioca doesn't have any flavor; the experience starts out bland but then immediately explodes with flavor—an amazing surprise. This version is far more elevated than in the market because we are going to be generous with the amount of filling and its size.

Unlike other dumplings, there is no need for folding and pinching. The trick here is to build the dough around the filling, then just do a gentle rolling. Roll all your stresses away.

If you're having trouble handling the dough, wear latex gloves so it's easy for you to roll. Make sure the dough is wet, but don't let the pieces touch each other because they will stick together.

### STUFFING

¼ cup canola or vegetable oil

2 (70g) discs palm sugar or ½ cup brown sugar

2 tablespoons granulated sugar

5 garlic cloves, finely chopped

2 tablespoons finely chopped cilantro stems

2 tablespoons finely chopped shallot

¼ cup finely chopped preserved sweet radish (from a Chinese grocery store)

6 ounces ground pork

2 tablespoons fish sauce

1½ teaspoons ground white pepper

1½ teaspoons freshly ground black pepper

½ cup crushed unsalted roasted peanuts

Big pinch of kosher salt

¼ cup chopped fresh cilantro leaves

### DUMPLINGS

Lettuce, napa cabbage, or banana leaves, for steaming

Cooking spray

1½ cups small white tapioca pearls (not the big dark ones for boba tea)

1 cup lukewarm water

### FOR SERVING

2 tablespoons Garlic Oil (page 45)

Butter lettuce leaves

Sliced red long hot chilies

Chopped fresh cilantro

Sliced cucumbers

Fried Garlic (optional; page 45)

1   Make the stuffing: In a deep nonstick skillet, combine the oil, palm sugar, granulated sugar, garlic, cilantro stems, and shallot. Cook over high heat, stirring, for 1 to 2 minutes. Add the sweet radish, ground pork, fish sauce, white pepper, and black pepper. Cook, breaking up the meat with a wooden spoon, until the color deepens, the meat is caramelized, and there is no more liquid in the pan, about 3 minutes. Stir in the peanuts, salt, and cilantro leaves and remove the pan from the heat. Spread the meat mixture on a plate and let it cool completely. You should have about 2 cups of filling.

2   Make the dumplings: Set up a steamer and fill it with 2 or 3 inches of water, but not so much that it comes up to the bottom of the basket or rack. Line the steamer basket with your leaves of choice and spray the tops of the leaves with cooking spray.

*recipe continues*

3 Put the tapioca pearls in a medium bowl, pour in the warm water, and mix gently with your hands. Press a piece of plastic wrap on the top of the tapioca and set aside for 5 minutes, or until you're done forming the filling.

4 Form the filling into 1-teaspoon balls and place them on a cutting board or clean work surface. (Or, if you have time, roll the filling into balls, freeze them until solid on a baking sheet, and keep them in a zip-top bag in the freezer. This lets you make these dumplings quickly, and makes them easier to form.)

5 Fill a small bowl with water and have it nearby. Wet your hands, measure 2 teaspoons of the tapioca onto the palm of one hand, and use the fingers of your other hand to flatten it across your palm and about half of the length of your fingers in a thin, even layer. If the tapioca isn't soft enough to flatten into a white paste, sprinkle it with a little water. Put a ball of filling on top of the flattened dough, then curl up your fingers to wrap the ball with the dough. Use the fingers on your other hand to press the dough all the way around the filling until it looks like a golf ball. Repeat with the remaining pork balls and tapioca.

6 Working in batches, arrange the tapioca balls in the steamer basket, keeping them apart so they don't stick together.

7 Bring the water in the steamer to a boil over high heat. Put the basket in the steamer, cover, and steam until the tapioca is translucent, 5 to 7 minutes over high heat.

8 **To serve:** Pour the garlic oil into a large shallow bowl. Add the steamed tapioca balls and turn to coat them in the oil. Serve over lettuce leaves with the chilies, cilantro, sliced cucumbers, and a sprinkling of fried garlic (if using).

# SEN MEE NAM SAI

## noodles *with* clear broth, spareribs & blood cubes

There will be blood!

This is a simple, clean noodle soup that is part of a Trang breakfast, with lots of nutrition from the spareribs, broth, and blood to start your day. Instead of taking iron pills, we eat blood, which actually doesn't have a strong flavor and has a texture like tender tofu. The soup is a clean, clear pork broth, a little salty and peppery, and you can choose your own adventure by seasoning the soup with different toppings and sauces like fried garlic, fish sauce, chili vinegar, or more chili flakes as you go.

If you are unfamiliar with blood in food, know that in many different cultures, there is the culinary use of blood—black pudding in England, boudin noir in France, soondae in Korea. In the old days, you would buy the whole animal and use every part of it to eat and make things from.

This dish tastes like home to me. Hello, home!

½ pound coagulated pig's blood, cut into 1-inch cubes (see Note)

1 pound pork spareribs

3½ tablespoons kosher salt

Handful of fresh cilantro stems

8 garlic cloves, smashed and peeled

1½ tablespoons sugar

1 tablespoon fish sauce

2 teaspoons ground white pepper

Rice noodles, cooked according to package directions, for serving

Chili and Vinegar Relish (page 42, Prik Dong), for serving

Fried Garlic, homemade (page 45) or store-bought, for serving

1  Gently rinse the blood cubes under cold running water. Bring a medium saucepan of water to a boil over high heat. Add the blood cubes and boil until they are nice and firm, 5 to 7 minutes, using a spoon to skim any foamy brown scum off the top of the water. Drain in a colander and rinse well under cold running water. Put the blood cubes in a medium bowl, cover with cold water, and set aside.

2  In a large pot, combine the spareribs, 2 tablespoons of the salt, and cold water to cover. Bring to a boil over high heat, skimming brown stuff off the top of the water as it forms. Then immediately turn off the heat. Drain the ribs in a colander and rinse under cold running water. This makes sure that the soup is clean of scum (so you don't have to skim the top of the soup as it cooks).

3  In a medium pot, combine 6 cups water, the ribs, cilantro stems, and garlic, adding more water if needed to fully submerge the ribs. Set over high heat, and when the liquid starts to bubble, add the remaining 1½ tablespoons salt and the sugar. Reduce the heat to low and cook until the ribs are tender, about 45 minutes.

4  Drain the blood cubes, rinse them one more time, and add them to the soup. Increase the heat to high and let the soup come to a bubble. Then stir in the fish sauce and white pepper and remove the pot from the heat.

5  Divide the soup among bowls and serve with rice noodles, chili and vinegar relish, and fried garlic.

NOTE: You can get pork blood cubes prepared at the Asian grocery. There is a belief that we should eat pork blood during a full moon because that's when it's very good quality and it coagulates very well and there will be no air bubbles.

# KANOM JEEB
## steamed pork, shrimp & crab dumplings

MAKES 12 DUMPLINGS

When I was very young, my uncle owned a fighting rooster ring, and we would feed the roosters with dumplings so they would be strong fighters. Rooster fighting is part of the culture across Southeast Asia.

Kanom jeeb is a bite-size open-top shumai-style dumpling, filled with savory pork, shrimp, and crab, that is always served at cafés in Trang. I used to make these dumplings in Philadelphia when I missed my mom. Any food that gets me closer to her, I will make it. Because people love them, at my restaurant we make three to four hundred in one go, but I'm only asking you to make twelve! Of course, you don't have to do this alone: you can double or triple the recipe or more and have a dumpling-wrapping party with a big bowl of filling and store-bought wonton wrappers. Make a bunch, freeze them, and steam them when you need it. It might take making a few of these before you get into a rhythm of wrapping them easily. But don't worry, you just need to think of the wrapper as a pouch; no need to stress about correct folds or pleats. It's going to look and taste good.

The recipe is set to make just twelve dumplings, which is great for a bite or two per person for a dinner party. But you can multiply it as much as you want. When you cook, it's always a time of joy when we stuff the dumplings and then eat together. There is no dumpling count per person. We eat as much as we like, and when we cook, that is our family time. Enjoy your family time. Celebrate love and feel satisfied. These dumplings are perfect served with tea for breakfast.

### NOK'S PORK, SHRIMP & CRAB FILLING
4 ounces shrimp, peeled and deveined, tails removed
4 ounces ground pork
½ teaspoon cornstarch
½ tablespoon finely chopped garlic
1 tablespoon finely chopped fresh cilantro
1 tablespoon finely sliced scallions
1 tablespoon sesame oil
1 tablespoon light brown sugar
Pinch of kosher salt
½ tablespoon freshly ground black pepper
½ tablespoon oyster sauce
½ tablespoon soy sauce
2 heaping tablespoons canned jumbo lump crabmeat

### DUMPLINGS
Parchment paper or butter lettuce leaves, for lining the steamer
12 round wonton wrappers, thawed if frozen
12 lumps jumbo lump crabmeat, for topping the dumplings

### FOR SERVING
Butter lettuce leaves
Thinly sliced scallions
Sriracha sauce
Garlic Oil (page 45)

1 **Make the filling:** Roughly chop the shrimp with a large chef's knife or cleaver. Then whack the pieces with the side of the knife to flatten them.

2 In a medium bowl, combine the smashed shrimp, ground pork, cornstarch, garlic, cilantro, scallions, sesame oil, brown sugar, salt, pepper, oyster sauce, and soy sauce. Use your hands to mix everything together. Add the crabmeat and mix gently, just until the crab is evenly distributed. Cover the bowl and refrigerate for 45 minutes or up to overnight.

*recipe continues*

3   **Make the dumplings:** Find a plate that fits inside a large steamer basket and line it with parchment paper or butter lettuce leaves.

4   Working one at a time, moisten the edges of a wonton wrapper with a little water and place it flat in the palm of one hand. Scoop about 1 tablespoon of the meat mixture into the center of the wonton wrapper. Then gather up the edges of the wonton around the filling, leaving the meat exposed on top. Make a ring around the top of the wonton pouch with your forefinger and thumb and squeeze gently to secure the shape, using the forefinger of your other hand to pack the filling into the pouch, but keeping the top of the pouch open—you should be able to see the filling. Gently press the bottom of the stuffed wonton onto your counter so it won't roll around in the steamer, then place it on the lined plate. Repeat with the rest of the filling and wonton wrappers.

5   When all of the wonton wrappers are stuffed and on the plate, dip your fingertips in water and moisten the tops of the pouches to help keep them closed while they steam. Press a lump of crabmeat into the top of each dumpling. Carefully lower the plate into your steamer basket.

6   Fill the steamer pot with 2 or 3 inches of water and place it over high heat. When the water begins to boil, set the steamer basket with the filled dumplings in the pot and cover with the lid. Steam on high until the filling is firm and cooked through (a sharp paring knife should come out clean when you insert it into the meat), 7 to 10 minutes.

7   **To serve:** Line a platter with fresh butter lettuce leaves. Using tongs, carefully transfer the steamed dumplings to the platter, sprinkle them with thinly sliced scallions, dot each one with some sriracha sauce, and drizzle a little garlic oil over top.

# HOO MOO PAK BOONG
## sweet & tart pig's ears

**SERVES 4 TO 6**

People have been eating all parts of the pig forever. You might not be familiar with it, but that's okay. You are adventurous, you are sophisticated, you love sustainability.

Pig ear is mellow in flavor, and here it's sweet and tart from the vinegar and the texture is crunchy and refreshing. The cucumbers paired with the dish are cool and refreshing, and the morning glory is green and earthy. If you don't want to cook your own pig ear, you can find pig ear that has been braised in five spice powder at the Chinese grocery store.

4 pig's ears

3 cinnamon sticks

3 star anise pods

5 whole cloves

5 large garlic cloves, peeled but whole

2 tablespoons Thai black soy sauce

2 tablespoons soy sauce

1 tablespoon kosher salt

2 tablespoons light brown sugar

**SAUCE**

¼ cup Sweet Chili Sauce (page 41, Nam Jim Waan)

¼ cup distilled white vinegar

1 tablespoon tomato paste

2 tablespoons granulated sugar

Pinch of kosher salt

**FOR SERVING**

½ cup coconut milk

1 seedless cucumber, diced or chopped

Morning glory or spinach (½ cup per person)

¼ cup chopped peanuts

1   Rinse the pig's ears under cool running water and snip off any hair.

2   In a large pot, combine 10 cups water, the cinnamon sticks, star anise, cloves, garlic, black soy sauce, regular soy sauce, salt, and brown sugar. Add the cleaned ears to the pot and bring to a boil over high heat. Reduce the heat to low and cook until the ears are tender (a sharp paring knife will easily slide in and out), 1½ to 2 hours.

3   Remove the pig's ears from the pot and discard the broth (or freeze it to use later for soup). Thinly slice the pig's ears and put them in a shallow bowl.

4   Make the sauce: In a small saucepan, combine the sweet chili sauce, vinegar, tomato paste, granulated sugar, and salt. Bring to a boil over high heat, stirring, then pour the sauce into a small bowl.

5   To serve: Rinse out the same small saucepan, pour in the coconut milk, and place it over medium heat. When the coconut milk is hot but not yet boiling, turn off the heat.

6   Top the sliced pig's ears with the cucumber, morning glory, and peanuts. Spoon some of the sauce over top and drizzle with the warm coconut milk. Serve immediately.

# YUM

**I won't apologize for saying it: What often passes as salad in North America can be depressing, whether it's a heap of wilted vegetables or noodles smothered in mayonnaise.**

But these spectacular Thai salads, known as yum, are bright, hearty, and zesty and will make you feel satisfied and hungry for more at the same time. Yum combines protein, vegetables, herbs, and spice, and can also include noodles or rice. You will never leave the table feeling hungry or sad because you chose salad.

A lot of Thai salads you may have encountered—like papaya salad, known as som tum, or different kinds of meat salads called larb—originate from Northeast, North, and Central Thailand. But the salads in this chapter have a Southern accent because they have been in my family for a long time, like the Khao Yum Kamin (page 104, Southern Thai Turmeric Rice Salad) my great-grandmother used to make, or because of the generous way I use spices and aromatics in Yum Nua (page 91, Steak Salad with Toasted Rice Powder). *Bon Appétit* and my husband both think it's amazing, and you will, too. When I came to America, the ingredients were different for me. The meat wasn't the same, the herbs and certain spices just didn't taste like what I was used to. I had to spend a long time trying to figure out the balance of ingredients.

While I encourage you to make these dishes the first time exactly according to recipes, consider Southern Thai salad as fashion: You dress it to impress, to your own style. When my gorgeous Pomeranian, Titi, picks out my outfits (he loves Issey Miyake), I can still accessorize them how I want. That's how I want you to treat these recipes.

# YUM WOON SEN TALAY/MOO SAAP
## glass noodle salad *with* shrimp, pork & squid

SERVES 4 TO 6 AS A MAIN DISH

I think this may just become your favorite salad of all time. Each bite of this is a dream, as the bounce of glass noodle, shrimp, and squid come together. (The *talay* in the title means "sea.") There is crunch from the roasted cashews, the aroma of fried garlic, and a savory quality to the pork. I often make this as an alternative to pasta because of how satisfying this dish is. There is a depth from the fried shallots, fried garlic, and dried shrimp, which gives it umami; there is a brightness from the lime juice, and the combination of dried and fresh chilies gives it a sweet heat.

As you read the recipe, you might feel intimidated because there seem to be a lot of steps, and it's true that this recipe is not one of the quick meals I've promised you. But listen to me: Nothing is difficult here; it's really about getting your mise en place together. That means having all of your ingredients measured and prepared before you start cooking. Whether you chop and fry the ingredients beforehand and come back to it, or do it all at once, the effort will pay off. Didn't I say this might become your favorite salad of all time?

Like with so many things, you can adjust this recipe as you like. You can leave out the chilies if you don't want the heat. You can make this vegan by using assorted mushrooms or fried tofu instead of pork and seafood, and by using soy sauce instead of fish sauce. You will find yourself sneaking forkfuls of this from the fridge!

If you're making this ahead of time, leave the cashews and fried onion out until it's time to serve, to keep their crunchiness. Glass noodles cook in under a minute, so make sure you cook them just until they are translucent and springy. If you have leftover glass noodles, you can use sauces from the Building Blocks chapter to dress them for an instant meal.

6½ ounces (180g) glass noodles

1 cup plus 3 tablespoons canola or vegetable oil

¼ cup finely chopped garlic

½ cup (50g) dried shrimp

½ pound ground pork

1 cup peeled and deveined medium shrimp, tails on

3 tablespoons fish sauce

1 pound squid, cleaned, trimmed, and cut into ½-inch-thick rings

½ cup cashews

8 Thai chilies, red and green, thinly sliced

1 cup thinly sliced scallions

½ cup packed chopped fresh cilantro

½ cup Seafood Sauce (page 34, Nam Jim Seafood)

2 tablespoons red chili flakes

2 to 3 teaspoons kosher salt

1 tablespoon sugar

½ cup fresh lime juice (about 4 limes)

1 cup halved cherry tomatoes

2 stalks roughly chopped Chinese celery (see Note, page 154)

2 tablespoons fried onion or shallots, store-bought or homemade (page 45)

*recipe continues*

1   Soak the glass noodles in a large bowl of warm water for 10 minutes. Drain.

2   In a small saucepan or skillet, heat ½ cup of the oil over high heat and right away add the chopped garlic. Let the garlic come to a sizzle; then keep cooking, stirring frequently, until it reaches a deep golden color, but do not let it get dark brown, as it will burn easily from there. This will take a couple of minutes; just keep a close eye on it. Pour ¼ cup of the fried garlic and oil into a small heatproof bowl; pour the rest into another sealable heatproof container to keep for future uses. (It can be stored indefinitely in the fridge.)

3   Pour another ½ cup of the oil into the same saucepan or skillet and set it over high heat. Add the dried shrimp and cook just until they turn golden in color, just a few moments. Then turn off the heat and keep stirring until the shrimp are evenly browned, 1 or 2 minutes. Use a slotted spoon to transfer the shrimp to paper towels to drain. Discard the oil or pour it into a jar to use for another meal.

4   In a medium pot, bring 8 cups water to a boil over high heat. Use clean kitchen shears to cut the soaked and drained glass noodles (keep them long; just run through them a couple times with the scissors) and drop them into the boiling water. Cook just until the noodles are translucent, about 1 minute. Drain the noodles very well and transfer them to another bowl. Toss the noodles with the reserved ¼ cup fried garlic and oil.

5   While you wait for the water to boil for the noodles, in a large skillet, heat 2 tablespoons of the oil over high heat. Add the pork and ¼ cup water. Cook, stirring and breaking up the meat (you're not trying to brown the meat). After a minute or two, add the shrimp and 1 tablespoon of the fish sauce. Cook, continuing to break up the meat into little bits, until the pork is cooked through and the shrimp is just firm, 2 to 3 more minutes. Transfer the meat and shrimp to a large bowl.

6   Add 1 tablespoon oil to the same skillet, still over high heat, and pour in ¼ cup water. When the water boils, add the squid and cook, stirring, just until it is firm and opaque, a few minutes. Turn off the heat and transfer the squid to a plate.

7   In a small dry skillet, toast the cashews over high heat just until you can smell them and they begin to brown. Put them in a bowl and set aside.

8   Dump the seasoned noodles into the bowl with the pork and shrimp. Add the Thai chilies, scallions, cilantro, seafood sauce, chili flakes, salt, sugar, lime juice, and remaining 2 tablespoons fish sauce. Using a large spoon, stir everything together and cut the noodles into smaller pieces if necessary. Add the squid, cherry tomatoes, and Chinese celery. Stir one more time. (Or put on gloves and use your hands to gently mix the ingredients together.)

9   Top with the fried dried shrimp, toasted cashews, and fried onion and serve. (If making ahead, leave these last garnishes off until ready to serve.)

# YUM NUA
## steak salad *with* toasted rice powder

SERVES 6 TO 8 AS A MAIN DISH WITH STICKY RICE OR 8 TO 10 AS PART OF A LARGER MEAL

I am about to cure your low iron levels and make you very happy. Yum nua is a crunchy and nourishing salad that gives you energy and makes you feel powerful. There is a spicy fiery bite, but don't be afraid, the flavors all come together. The steak used in this salad becomes bright from the addition of lemongrass, lime, and cucumbers, and the earthy vegetable flavors are not overpowered by spice. The toasted rice powder adds a subtle smokiness and crunch; don't skip this!

I encourage you to mix vegetables from your garden or the farmers' market into this salad and see where it takes you, even if the vegetables are not typically Thai. That is the spirit in which I cook, too; sometimes I want to preserve how things are done, and sometimes I feel free to adapt to what is available and fresh. I love serving this salad for lunch on a warm summer day because it fills you up without feeling heavy.

When you are making this, remember that the chef's hand is the chef's best tool; we want all the ingredients to be mixed in. Toss, do not squeeze, and this is how you are meant to use your hands. God gave you hands to make yum.

### BEEF
- ½ cup fish sauce
- 2 tablespoons granulated sugar
- ½ cup plus 3 tablespoons vegetable oil
- 1½ to 2 tablespoons kosher salt
- 2 teaspoons freshly ground black pepper
- 2 teaspoons ground white pepper
- 2 pounds skirt steak

### DRESSING
- 2 tablespoons fresh lime juice
- ½ cup Seafood Sauce (page 34, Nam Jim Seafood)
- 1 tablespoon fish sauce
- 2 tablespoons red chili flakes
- 2 to 3 teaspoons kosher salt
- 2 tablespoons light brown sugar

### SALAD
- 1½ cups thinly sliced shallots (about 6 medium shallots)
- 2 fresh lemongrass stalks, tender white parts only (see page 17), very thinly sliced
- 1 pint cherry tomatoes, halved
- 1 large cucumber, peeled, halved lengthwise, seeded, and cut into ¼-inch-thick half-moons
- 6 scallions, trimmed and thinly sliced
- 2 red long hot chilies, thinly sliced, plus more for garnish
- 5 garlic cloves, thinly sliced
- 1 cup fresh mint leaves
- 2 cups fresh cilantro leaves with tender stems, chopped, some leaves reserved for garnish
- 3 tablespoons fresh lime juice (about 1½ limes)
- 2 tablespoons Toasted Rice Powder (page 18), plus more for garnish
- Lime wedges, for serving

*recipe continues*

1   **Prepare the beef:** In a large bowl, whisk together the fish sauce, granulated sugar, ½ cup of the oil, salt, black pepper, and white pepper. Add the skirt steak and turn to coat it in the marinade. Let the steak marinate for at least 1 hour at room temperature, or cover and refrigerate overnight.

2   Take the meat out of the marinade. Place a large cast-iron skillet over high heat. When the pan begins to smoke, add the remaining 3 tablespoons oil and let it get very hot. Then, when the oil is just beginning to smoke, add half of the beef, making sure it is spread out in a single layer; don't crowd the pan (if you have a smaller skillet, you'll want to work in three or four batches, cutting the meat if necessary). Cook the steak until charred but medium-rare in the center, about 2 minutes per side. Transfer it to a plate to rest for 5 minutes. Repeat with the remaining steak.

3   When all the beef has rested for 5 minutes, slice it thinly against the grain and place it in a large serving bowl.

4   **Make the dressing:** In a small bowl, stir together the lime juice, seafood sauce, fish sauce, chili flakes, salt, and brown sugar. Add to the beef and gently mix with your hands until the beef is evenly coated.

5   **Assemble the salad:** Add the shallots and most of the lemongrass (reserve a tablespoon of lemongrass for garnish) to the beef and gently mix with your hands until everything is evenly incorporated. Add the tomatoes and cucumber and gently mix the ingredients together again. Add the scallions, chilies, garlic, and most of the mint (reserve 6 to 8 mint leaves for garnish) and gently mix again. Add the cilantro to the salad. Add the lime juice and rice powder and gently mix the salad one more time.

6   Garnish the salad with a sprinkling of rice powder, the reserved lemongrass, mint leaves, red hot chilies, and cilantro. Serve immediately with lime wedges.

# YUM HED RUAM
## scared mushroom salad

SERVES 4 AS PART OF A LARGER MEAL OR WITH STICKY RICE

This is a light and simple salad that is super healthy and comes together in less than fifteen minutes. It has an herbaceous flavor that comes from the cilantro, mint, and scallions. A warm comfort rises from the mushrooms and soy sauce, and a beautiful heat from the chilies complements any other dish you serve. I use local assorted mushrooms, but use whatever mushrooms you can find. You will feel so proud of yourself for making this salad and still have time for your self-care.

But before your self-care, imagine me screaming (gently) at you: "Never wash your mushrooms!" Just brush the dirt off. Please and thank you.

2 tablespoons canola or vegetable oil

8 large garlic cloves, 5 finely chopped, 3 thinly sliced

1 pound assorted mushrooms, stemmed and cut into ½- to 1-inch chunks

2 tablespoons soy sauce

Kosher salt

Ground white pepper

Freshly ground black pepper

2 tablespoons fresh lime juice

1 teaspoon red chili flakes

4 Thai chilies, thinly sliced, plus more for garnish

2 tablespoons thinly sliced shallot

2 tablespoons thinly sliced fresh mint leaves, plus more for garnish

4 medium scallions, thinly sliced

¼ cup chopped fresh cilantro

1   In a large deep skillet, heat the oil over high heat until it starts to smoke. Add the chopped garlic and mushrooms, stir to coat in the oil, then add 1 tablespoon of the soy sauce, a big pinch of salt, and a pinch each of white and black pepper. Cook, stirring, just until the mushrooms are tender, about 2 minutes. Transfer the mushroom mixture to a large bowl to cool to room temperature.

2   Add the lime juice, remaining 1 tablespoon soy sauce, chili flakes, sliced garlic, Thai chilies, shallot, mint, scallions, and cilantro to the mushrooms. Toss well.

3   Serve garnished with more fresh mint and thinly sliced Thai chilies.

# THE MARKETS ALL DAY

Even before the roosters start crowing in Yan Ta Khao, I am awake and ready to go. My phone says it's 4 a.m., and I grab my shopping basket and walk to the morning market before all the good stuff is sold out. Vendors from across the city have been setting up since 2 a.m. and sell the freshest and most exciting products of the day, fish, meat, and herbs, breakfast and snacks. It's so early because many of the vendors are farmers or other workers who must "start" their day after many hours of working at the market. To miss this market is to miss the best of the day; if you get here at 6 a.m., you are too late.

Workers and professionals can get their breakfast here, and home cooks and food stall owners can find the best ingredients for their cooking that day. As I walk through the market, my senses start waking up. I can see the tent lights illuminating the herbs and chilies to look their very best. I can hear the cleaver cutting through fresh pork and smell the licorice scent of Thai basil and frying curry paste.

Everything in the market sparks joy for me: the bursts of fire from woks, and pots simmering to make a gentle and flavorful breakfast, and the smoke of charcoal grills cooking marinated meat low and slow. There is something special about being able to talk to your vendors and build a relationship, something special about being able to touch your produce and your fish so you know that you are getting the best. We don't plan our meals through the week, we cook with our intuition and cook based on the ingredients that are best that day.

I used to wake up and come here with my mom to buy crab before they exported the picked meat to other cities in Thailand. We are a coastal area, so we eat wild-caught and hook-and-line seafood; the seafood is always so fresh and vibrant. It hasn't been flown across the world—it's true sea-to-table eating.

The morning market activates the senses, from the buttery aroma of Thai crullers known as pa thong go frying in vats of oil, to the honey-vinegar smell of ripening fruit, and the clean grassy scent of fresh grouper, white and red snapper, carp on ice. There are blue and pink plastic bins of fresh crabs trying to climb out and run from their fate, and mirror-like squid that will be grilled later. There are bunches of neatly bundled basil, curry leaves, and cilantro where the abundance of green feels like the jungle.

I stop at a stand selling Kanom Jeen (page 65, Rice Noodles with Coconut Fish Curry), and then I pick up some mango and papaya to cut at home and find the freshly butchered beef for tonight's meal.

When I pass my baht to the hands of the people who caught my fish, butchered my meat, and harvested my herbs, I am connected to a cycle of community and a tradition of people who know where ingredients come from. Each community of workers—from the fishermen and the butchers to the farmers and gardeners—is reflected here. The market gives people an opportunity to show their skill, whether they grow their own herbs from the garden or pick the best seafood from the fisherman.

When the sun starts to rise, most of the vendors start to clean the stalls and pack up for harvesting and fishing for the next day. For me, it's the time to sit and have a coffee and get other errands done or see my family. The afternoon market will start soon enough, which is filled with snacks and curries, and then the evening market, which is always a good stop for dinner. Even though there is a big shiny grocery store and convenience stores are popping up all over the South, people will always prefer the community and camaraderie of the market.

Now, at home in Philadelphia, I realize I don't have a Thai market across the street. You probably don't either. But that's okay, you can try for the same energy by talking to your local vendors. You can go to your farmers' market with your shopping bag and feel the same way I do, by learning about what people do. Talk to your butcher or fishmonger and your mushroom guy. Learn their names, learn about their work, learn about the produce or the protein. Even in the supermarket, you can talk with the butcher and the people working there, and make an adventure of seeking out your ingredients. Come back often and learn their names. This is how we create community (even if they won't let you touch the fish).

# GOONG CHAE NAM PLA
## raw white prawns *with* crunchy vegetables & spicy sauce

SERVES 4 TO 6

This dish is not truly considered a yum (a salad), but its freshness reminds me of the market. The minute the shrimp came from the ocean, my mother would go back home and make this right away. This is a simple ceviche-like dish, and the key here is using the freshest ingredients you can find so you can achieve the brightest balanced bite with fresh, sweet shrimp, crunchy ribbons of cabbage and bitter melon, and spicy, garlicky fish sauce.

The bitter melon and crunchy cabbage offset the spiciness of this beautiful dish. Take a bite of the bitter melon, a bite of the garlic, and make sure the shrimp is in the sauce. You will feel healthy and happy. Everyone will say "Wow!" Feel the burn! Everything is so fresh and herbaceous.

"Marinating" the raw shrimp in seltzer water makes the shrimp meat tighter and gives it an amazing crunch.

And yes, you can prepare ceviche at home. Just get the freshest shrimp you can find; if it smells good and sweet and like the clean ocean, it will be fine. I have seen where you get your happy hour sushi from, so no excuses.

12 jumbo shrimp, peeled and deveined, tails left on

1 (12-ounce) can unflavored seltzer

1½ tablespoons fish sauce

1 teaspoon granulated sugar

**FOR SERVING**

1 cup very thinly sliced green cabbage

½ cup Seafood Sauce (page 34, Nam Jim Seafood)

1 or 2 large garlic cloves, very thinly sliced

1 red long hot chili, very thinly sliced on the diagonal

½ cup cored and very thinly sliced bitter melon, soaked for a few minutes in cold water

6 to 8 fresh mint leaves

1  Put the shrimp in a bowl and pour the seltzer over top. Set aside for 5 minutes.

2  In a medium bowl, mix together the fish sauce and sugar.

3  Drain and squeeze the shrimp gently to remove excess moisture, pat them dry with paper towels, and add them to the bowl with the fish sauce/sugar mixture. Toss to coat the shrimp, then cover and freeze for 30 minutes. (This keeps the shrimp super cold and the flavor fresh; if it does freeze a little, the sauce will thaw it out.)

4  **To serve:** Mound the cabbage in the middle of a serving platter and arrange the shrimp around it in a circle. (If you want, cut a hole in each shrimp just below the tail and pull the tails through the body to make little swans.) Pour half of the seafood sauce over top and garnish with the garlic, chili, bitter melon, and mint. Serve with the remaining seafood sauce at the table, so guests can add more if they like.

# YUM MA KUER YAO

## spicy eggplant salad *with* chili jam & coconut cream

I call this my Thai baba ghanoush, and it shares many of the beautiful smoky, savory qualities of that dish, but with more meaty goodness from turkey and shrimp. (Of course, you can use tofu, or just leave these out, and use soy sauce instead of fish sauce to keep it vegetarian.) My family always ordered this at our favorite Chinese restaurant in Trang, and it reminds me of those special times of togetherness and love. Of course, the dish is more Thai than Chinese, so it's a little like when you go to a Chinese restaurant here and you love the chicken wings and French fries, but delicious food is delicious food. And I make my version more delicious and luxurious with more steps and more ingredients, because that's me, I'm extra. You can streamline it for yourself, but try it my way first!

Remember that Mom's Chili Jam (page 257, Nam Prik Phao) you made and have stocked in the fridge? It's time to use it! The dressing hits sweet, sour, and mild notes with just a bit of spice and makes the eggplant sweet and creamy. The lime juice and fish sauce add so much flavor. Coconut cream adds a depth and richness to the salad.

When I make it for guests, I grill the eggplant the night before and let it sit in lime juice and fish sauce to soak up all the flavor and make the salad even more delicious.

### EGGPLANT

4 medium Chinese eggplants

1 tablespoon fish sauce

1 tablespoon fresh lime juice

### DRESSING

⅓ cup coconut cream

¼ cup Mom's Chili Jam (page 257, Nam Prik Phao)

2 tablespoons tamarind concentrate (see page 22)

½ tablespoon fish sauce

½ tablespoon fresh lime juice

Kosher salt

### MEAT MIXTURE

½ pound ground turkey

4 ounces medium shrimp, peeled, deveined, tails off, and chopped (see Note; page 102)

2 tablespoons coconut cream

1 tablespoon canola or vegetable oil

1 teaspoon to ½ tablespoon kosher salt

1 tablespoon sugar

½ tablespoon fish sauce

2 tablespoons fresh lime juice

¼ cup thinly sliced shallots

2 tablespoons thinly sliced scallion

2 tablespoons chopped fresh cilantro

### FOR SERVING

1 or 2 red long hot chilies, thinly sliced on the diagonal

3 eggs, hard-boiled

½ cup coconut cream

1 tablespoon rice flour

2 tablespoons thinly sliced scallion

2 tablespoons fried onion or shallots, store-bought or homemade (page 45)

*recipe continues*

1  **Prepare the eggplant:** Preheat the broiler. Set the whole eggplants on a baking sheet and broil for 8 minutes. Flip them over and broil until they are wrinkly and soft and charred, about 8 more minutes. (Or you can grill them whole until tender.)

2  Remove from the oven, cover with a clean kitchen towel, and let them sit for 5 minutes. Carefully peel off the skins and put the naked eggplant on a platter. Use kitchen shears or a knife to take off the stem ends and cut the flesh into 2-inch pieces.

3  In a small bowl, stir together the fish sauce and lime juice. Drizzle the mixture over the eggplant, cover with plastic wrap, and let sit while you prepare the rest of the salad.

4  **Make the dressing:** In a small saucepan, combine the coconut cream and mom's chili jam (Nam Prik Phao). Cook over medium heat, breaking it up with a spoon until the jam is fully dissolved into the coconut cream and the liquid begins to bubble. Remove from the heat and stir in the tamarind concentrate, fish sauce, lime juice, and a big pinch of salt. Set aside.

5  **Make the meat mixture:** In a small bowl, use your hands to mix together the ground turkey and chopped shrimp.

6  In a medium saucepan, combine the coconut cream, oil, and ¼ cup water and set over medium-high heat Add the turkey and shrimp and cook, stirring to break up the turkey, until the meat is fully cooked, 3 to 5 minutes. Add the salt, sugar, fish sauce, lime juice, and the prepared dressing. Stir well and let the sauce bubble for 3 to 5 minutes, then stir in the shallots, scallions, and cilantro.

7  **To serve:** Place the prepared eggplant on a serving platter. Spoon the meat mixture over the eggplant and top with the sliced chilies. Cut the hard-boiled eggs into wedges and arrange them around the eggplant on the platter.

8  In a small saucepan, combine the coconut cream and rice flour and cook, stirring, over medium heat just until the mixture has thickened.

9  Drizzle the coconut cream over the eggplant and meat mixture. Garnish with the sliced scallion and fried shallots and serve.

NOTE: You can leave a few shrimp whole for a prettier presentation.

# YOU CAN'T HIDE THE TRUTH WITH SWEETNESS

Yum stalls are everywhere in Thailand, and they are much like a salad bar: You can add ingredients to your preference. When you have a good salad on a hot day, you will know it; like when you have a great yum nua (steak salad), it's packed with protein and so you will be able to do heavy yard work or have a strong mind at your computer screen. Yum should always be nourishing and invigorating.

But when I travel back home, I've noticed a strong sweetness creeping into yum, and the balance of flavors is changing. Many vendors won't even use palm sugar anymore, unlike in the old days, when we used only the discs of palm sugar, which has a complex flavor. Now they just use simple syrup. Yum should actually start with lime juice and fish sauce, with sugar as just a minor part of the seasoning. When I get glass noodles that are too glossy, I know they put sugar in it and it's inedible to me. We are not making candy, we are making salad.

My mom also knows when there is too much sugar. Our dishes were always salty, sour, peppery, spicy, and creamy. If a salad is too sweet, it means you are getting lazy.

Sweet is attractive and is slowly making palates change. This could be because of a new generation's preference for sweetness, or the giant big-box stores and the 7-Eleven, with the convenience of packaged meals and some Western sweets, or the bakeries, or it could be because flavorful ingredients are getting more expensive. There are times where I go to a food stall with high hopes, and I feel disappointed that the depth of flavor is overpowered by sugar. It's an easy shortcut to make sales in a competitive market, but with that shift toward sweet, we lose the integrity and beauty of really great Thai food. The flavors must complement one another, and the ingredients should be subtle and distinguished, like the lime juice in a salad or the gentle contrast of an anchovy against cool raw vegetables.

In America, Thai restaurants often serve something that is unrecognizable as the food I grew up with. I think like so many immigrant communities that arrived here, when waves of Thai restaurants opened in the nineties, they were afraid to show the true potential of our food. I can't blame them, because their livelihoods depend on it; if a restaurant finds easy and cheap ways to fill people up with sugar and some MSG, then maybe somehow you will make a margin to survive the next day.

It's only starting to change here now. For every dozen restaurants that adjust the spice levels or dump sandcastles of sugar in their food, there is someone else who is trying to explore the greater potential of our flavors and challenge the notions of what it means to please an American palate. And diners are starting to become more sophisticated in what they expect or are more willing to be surprised (except for the ones that write crazy Google reviews).

Before I became a chef, I left my career as a flight attendant to start my life in the United States. Like so many who come here, I had to start over. I was a housewife trying to find my way in a new country, and I missed my home food. I didn't have access to my Trang market, I had my memories. It was hard to find good ingredients, it was hard to find the right ingredients, and there was so much trial and error. I would cook and share my food with my neighbors and friends, and it made me so happy when they said it was like nothing they ever tasted before.

This is all to say, you don't have to take shortcuts or sacrifice flavors. You don't have to give up when something doesn't come out right or hide in fear from the chilies. You can make my recipes at home and they can be complex, bold, and true.

# KHAO YUM KAMIN
## southern thai turmeric rice salad

SERVES 5 TO 8 AS PART OF A LARGER MEAL

I re-created this salad after my visit to Phuket with Philadelphia food critic Craig Laban. I remembered how my great-grandmother used to make this for me when I was a young girl and how comforted I felt when eating it. I'm writing this cookbook because recipes sometimes get lost with time. My mom did not remember this recipe, so I had to re-create it from my own memory so I could continue to share it. I hope it's something you will pass down to the next generation, too!

There are a lot of variations of Southern Thai turmeric rice salad, but this version is uniquely my own. The lime juice adds an extra dimension, and the citrus melds with the coconut. When plated, this salad is a rainbow: the yellow of the turmeric against green herbs, orange carrots, and purple cabbage, and the silvery anchovies shine by adding crunchy umami. You want to make sure to get the rice, herbs and vegetables in each bite of salad so you can experience your life to the fullest.

This is a fun recipe you can play around with; if you don't have one of the vegetables on the list, sub it for what you do have and make your own variation. Make it together with your family and friends so you can keep the memories for years to come.

If you tell me you don't like anchovies, you haven't tried good ones or probably haven't tried them at all. Dried anchovies are delicious and good for you. You need calcium! Trust me.

1½ cups jasmine rice

¼ cup Kalaya House Curry Paste (page 55)

1 teaspoon plus 1 tablespoon kosher salt

3¾ cups water

2 tablespoons sugar

1 tablespoon very thinly sliced makrut lime leaves

2 tablespoons canola or vegetable oil

¼ cup dried anchovies (see Note)

¾ cup unsweetened shredded coconut

¼ cup Ground Dried Shrimp (page 137)

¼ cup fresh lime juice (about 2 limes)

**FOR SERVING**

Shredded carrots and/or red cabbage

Long beans or green beans

Thinly sliced pineapple, mango, and/or pomelo

Bean sprouts

Fresh basil and/or mint leaves

Thinly sliced makrut lime leaves

1  Rinse the rice thoroughly in a fine-mesh sieve under cool running water, shake out the water, then dump the rice into a medium saucepan. Stir in the curry paste, 1 teaspoon of the salt, and the water, and bring to a boil over high heat. Reduce the heat to low, cover (preferably with a glass lid, so you can check on the rice without lifting the lid), and cook until the rice is tender, about 15 minutes. If the rice looks too dry or you smell it starting to burn on the bottom before the top grains are cooked, use a wooden spatula to scrape up the browned rice from the bottom of the pan, add 2 tablespoons or up to ¼ cup more water, then cover and steam for another 10 minutes. It's important that the cooked rice is nice and dry, so add the extra water only if you really have to.

2  Stir in the sugar, remaining 1 tablespoon salt, and lime leaves. Scoop the rice onto a large plate to cool to room temperature.

3   Meanwhile, in a medium skillet, heat the oil over high heat. Add the dried anchovies and fry, stirring, just until they dance in the skillet and begin to deepen in color, just a few minutes; keep an eye on them. Turn off the heat and keep stirring for about a minute to let the dried fish brown evenly, then transfer them to paper towels to drain.

4   Wipe out the skillet, add the coconut, and toast it over medium heat, stirring frequently, until it turns golden in color. Turn off the heat and keep stirring to deepen the color even more, then let it cool slightly and grind it to a coarse powder in a food processor or spice grinder, or with a mortar and pestle.

5   Add the ground coconut and ground dried shrimp to the rice and mix well. Add ¼ cup of the fried anchovies and the lime juice and mix again just until the fish are evenly distributed. (You can snack on the rest of the anchovies or store them indefinitely in an airtight container.)

6   Divide the rice mixture among eight 4-ounce or five 6-ounce ramekins or bowls, pressing down to pack it in tightly. Invert one serving of rice onto the center of a plate and arrange the raw vegetables all around to serve.

NOTE: These are not the canned or salted anchovies you get in Italian or European markets; look for dried anchovies in the Asian market; they will be silvery and almost crispy.

# KAENG

**Southern Thai curries are bold, fiery, and layered. They are made from pounded aromatic pastes and dry spice blends that are combined with coconut milk, water, or stock.**

The herbs and spices that create the base for curry paste are what make it exceptional, and the nuanced bold flavors awaken your brain to how complex and good a curry can be. The recipes in this chapter feature a range of flavor profiles, from the warm anise and cinnamon of massaman curry to the herby brightness of green curry to the spicy sweet tones of pineapple tofu curry.

Curry is comfort food, and it's food to awaken your senses and spirit. But one thing curry is not, is soup, unlike what many of the watery takeout curries you see might make you think. It isn't a dip. It is *not* meant to be eaten by itself. And please don't dump your rice into the curry. When I see someone dump their rice into the curry or order the curry as their sole lonely entrée, I take them by the hand, I look them in the eyes, and I say "Let me show you how to enjoy curry," and send out a fresh curry, rice, and an accompaniment like my Three-Ingredient Cabbage (page 186, Kalum Thod Nam Pla) or a bright crunchy salad like Khao Yum Kamin (page 104, Southern Thai Turmeric Rice Salad).

Curry is meant to be spooned over rice with thoughtfulness and grace, and combined with crunchy cooling flavors such as cucumbers, radishes, long beans, carrots, salads, and stir-fries. That's one of the things I really want people to know about Thai food: Most dishes are best enjoyed with contrasting flavors from *other* dishes or from the platters of crunchy raw vegetables and herbs that we serve on the table. (You'll find suggestions for recipes in the book to be served together in our pairing menus on page 278.) Curry makes you happy, but if you make a big bowl of curry and eat it without accompaniments, you will be sad. You will be missing the party. And you will write a bad review of this book.

When people say they don't like curry, I say, "If you don't like my curry when you eat it in my restaurant, I won't take your money."

But still, some people insist they don't like curry because they had a bad curry—maybe it was full of mushy overcooked vegetables and stiff, overcooked meat. Or maybe they had all the different kinds of curry, but these curries were so flavorless that they couldn't tell their tastes apart.

We need to get over the color wheel of curry (red, yellow, green) that everyone is so used to and consider what makes curry special. You have to make curry with real ingredients, including the best curry paste, which is one you make yourself. (The homemade curry paste section, starting on page 50 will change your life.)

What makes these curries uniquely Southern is the amount of black pepper, white pepper, shrimp paste, makrut lime leaves, galangal, hometown curry powders, and dried spices. Sometimes people say that we in the South always have a heavy hand with our spices . . . and you should, too. Curries steal the show on the Southern Thai table, and eating them makes you feel alive because of the layers of flavor. These recipes are noted for their different intensities, from mild to spicy.

This chapter is filled with an unforgettable creamy-sweet and spicy Gaeng Gai Khao Mun (page 114, Southern-Style Chicken Curry) paired with Green Coconut Rice (page 235), the most fragrant and bubbly Chicken Panang Curry (page 121, Panang Gai) you've ever seen, and surprising curries, including Steamed Pork and Crabmeat Curry (page 136, Hor Mok Moo) that uses a technique that may challenge everything you know about curry.

Don't feel intimidated, you can handle this. I'm going to hold your hand. We are going on this journey together. Let's do this.

And here's my first hand-hold: It is good to have a 10- to 12-inch steamer pot or steaming rack, a wok or a heavy skillet, and a Dutch oven for most of these recipes. See the equipment list (pages 12 to 13).

# NOK'S TIPS FOR MAKING AND SERVING CURRY

- If you don't have coconut cream, pour a can of coconut milk into a wide jar or clear container. Leave it in the fridge for a few hours and skim the cream off the top. The rest you can freeze and use for the next time you make curry.

- Stirring the curry and scraping the sides and the bottom of the pan will prevent it from scorching, especially for long-cooking curries like Spicy Celebration Goat Curry (page 132, Kang Pae).

- The oil separating at the top is a great sign that the flavors have developed.

- I prefer to cook curry in a 5-quart Dutch oven. If the pot you use is bigger, it might over-reduce. If it's narrower and deeper, then you will need to reduce longer.

- If you are done cooking curry and it still looks too watery, take the protein out and reduce the curry more until you see the sheen, then add the protein back in.

- If you over-reduce the curry, add a bit more water or coconut milk.

- Lime leaves can be difficult to find in places, but when you find them, keep them in your freezer in an airtight Ziploc bag.

- The freshest herbs we can get our hands on are Thai basil leaves. Thai basil is affordable and has a tropical note. We aren't focused on the holy trinity of basils here (Thai basil, holy basil, lemon basil). Regular sweet basil is fine, too, if you can't access Thai basil.

- Basil is used as a green, and you want to keep that beautiful green color. So stir just to combine and turn off the heat so you don't cook it too long.

- The house-made curry paste can be a little chunky, and it gives a nice body to the curry. Do not worry if your curry is not as smooth as a store-bought curry sauce. It's nice to bite into the aromatics.

- Spoon the curry over the rice a little at a time. Every day at my restaurant, I see someone dump their rice into the curry, and I reach out and hold their hand. I fish out the rice and give them a fresh entree because mixing rice and curry together is not the right thing to do. You can't appreciate the layers of flavor in the food; it won't taste the same. The curry should be spooned over the rice so the flavors are introduced slowly, and because the rice has its own unique flavor and serves as a vehicle for multiple dishes on the Southern Thai table. Southern Thai food is meant to be eaten with rice. The good carbs from rice are not a bad thing; rice is mandatory.

- Curry is usually not served as a one-plate meal in our culture. Definitely you want to eat it with rice, as a sauce for rice, but also with other dishes. In many of these recipes, I will offer suggestions for other dishes to serve them with, but a plate of crunchy, cold, raw or blanched vegetables like cucumbers, long beans, cabbage, or other veggies is always great to give you a cooling, fresh contrast to bite into.

# KUA GLING NUA

## *toasted beef curry, my favorite fiery curry*

SERVES 6 TO 8 WITH RICE, RAW VEGETABLES, AND OTHER DISHES

Let's turn up the heat! Pepper Curry Paste (page 50, Gaeng Kua Prig) is front and center in this dish. (You can also make it with any ground meat, not just beef.) Yes, it's very hot, but very herbaceous, and I hate when someone tries this dish and says: "This isn't for the faint of heart!" First, nobody's going to die from eating chilies. And kua gling nua is meant to be enjoyed *with* other dishes on the Southern Thai table, like My Mother's Caramelized Pork (page 175, Moo Waan), so its heat is not meant to overwhelm your meal. All you need is a tablespoon or two with rice and cooling vegetables like cucumbers, and it wakes up the whole meal with its intensity and flavor. Think of it as a combination of main course and condiment.

The other thing I want you to know about this curry is that it's dry—there is no sauce, but it's dry-roasted. *Kua* means "toasted," which means cooked slowly over low heat. *Gling* means "moving," so we keep the meat moving on the pan to avoid burning the paste until it's absorbed all the flavor from the seasonings.

The pepper will make you sneeze a lot and cry a little bit while you cook, but that's a sign you are going in the right direction.

2 tablespoons canola or vegetable oil

½ cup Pepper Curry Paste (page 50, Gaeng Kua Prig)

1 tablespoon shrimp paste

½ tablespoon freshly ground black pepper

½ tablespoon ground white pepper

1½ tablespoons red chili flakes

1 pound ground beef

1 tablespoon fish sauce

3 makrut lime leaves, very thinly sliced

2 red long hot chilies, thinly sliced on the diagonal

1 cup packed fresh basil leaves

1   In a large skillet, heat the oil over high heat until it just begins to smoke. Add the curry paste, shrimp paste, black pepper, white pepper, and chili flakes. Reduce the heat to medium. Stir with a wooden spoon until the shrimp paste is melted down and the mixture is fragrant, about 2 minutes. (When you start sneezing, that's when you know it's ready.)

2   Add the ground beef and ¼ cup water. Grab another wooden spoon and cook, breaking up the meat with both spoons, until the meat is no longer pink, 5 to 7 minutes. Add the fish sauce, increase the heat to medium-high, and cook, stirring frequently, until the meat looks a bit drier, about 3 more minutes. Stir in the lime leaves, chilies, and basil leaves. Stir-fry until the basil is wilted.

**Serve with:** Jasmine Rice (page 234) and raw vegetables or Moo Waan (page 175, My Mother's Caramelized Pork) or the Khai Jiew Samoun Prai (page 249, Cilantro, Basil, and Scallion Omelet).

# GAENG GAI KHAO MUN
## southern-style chicken curry

SERVES 6 TO 8

This is my great-grandmother's chicken curry recipe, and it's one of the most beloved dishes I cook. My family has loved it for generations. In Trang, we serve this as a summer lunch. The combination of shrimp paste, lime leaf, coconut cream, basil, black pepper, and the herby mellowness from lemongrass, galangal, and turmeric in the Kalaya curry paste make this dish essential Southern comfort food.

Southern-style chicken curry is perfectly balanced between creamy, sweet, and spicy flavors. It's fantastic paired with my Green Coconut Rice (page 235), whose pandan leaf and cilantro bring out the sweetness of the chicken curry and temper the heat. The coconut milk and coconut cream make the curry extremely decadent, so you don't need to eat a lot to feel full.

You will never think of chicken curry as "basic" again. Bring on the luxury!

¼ to ⅓ cup Kalaya House Curry Paste (page 55), to taste

1 tablespoon shrimp paste

3 tablespoons light brown sugar

1½ cups coconut cream

1 pound boneless, skinless chicken breasts, cut into 1-inch cubes

1 pound boneless, skinless chicken thighs, cut into 1-inch cubes

1 (13.5-ounce) can coconut milk

6 tablespoons fish sauce

1½ to 2 teaspoons kosher salt

1 teaspoon freshly ground black pepper

1 teaspoon ground white pepper

1 large bunch basil, leaves picked and soaked in cold water, stems discarded

7 makrut lime leaves, 5 torn, 2 leaves cut into chiffonade for garnish

2 red long hot chilies, thinly sliced

1 In a large pot or Dutch oven, combine the curry paste, shrimp paste, 2 tablespoons of the brown sugar, and ¾ cup of the coconut cream. Set the pot over medium-low heat and cook, breaking up the shrimp paste and whisking frequently, until the curry sauce is fragrant and bubbling and the shrimp paste is fully dissolved, 4 to 7 minutes. Cook this mixture low and slow so you don't burn the curry and shrimp pastes.

2 Add the chicken, increase the heat to high, and stir with a wooden spoon until all the chicken pieces are coated in the sauce. Pour in the coconut milk. When the mixture comes to a boil, reduce the heat to medium and cook until the chicken is tender and there is a darker yellow sheen on the top of the sauce, about 20 minutes.

3 Stir in the fish sauce and the remaining ¾ cup coconut cream. Increase the heat to medium-high and cook, stirring frequently, for 5 minutes to emulsify the cream into the sauce. Season with the salt, black pepper, white pepper, and the remaining 1 tablespoon brown sugar.

4 Drain the basil leaves and set aside 6 leaves for garnish. Add the rest to the pot, along with the torn makrut leaves. Stir well, then remove from the heat.

5 Transfer the curry to a serving bowl and garnish with the reserved basil leaves and the sliced chilies. Scatter the makrut leaf chiffonade on top.

**Serve with:** Green Coconut Rice (page 235).

# CAENG PU

## southern-style crab curry

SERVES 6

When you feel tired but also crave luxurious food, what should you do? (Haven't we all been there?) Make gaeng pu! This curry is easy to make even when you're exhausted.

If you have Kalaya curry paste premade and a can of crabmeat, you're ready to make this quick curry, where the curry paste and shrimp paste blend together beautifully with coconut milk, hitting sweet and peppery notes. Healthy and quick; eat it with rice, or it can make simple rice noodles and raw vegetables taste delicious.

At the market in Trang, we have an abundance of freshly caught and affordable seafood and what is available depends on the time of the day. When I was a child, my mom and I would wake up at 4 a.m. and go to the market to buy fresh picked crabmeat before it was sent to the city for export.

If you don't live near the ocean, I understand that access to fresh ingredients can vary depending on where you are located, and using canned lump crab is just as good. And while I believe in treating yourself, of course crab can be expensive. This recipe would also be delicious using chopped raw fish fillets or shrimp. Just cook them a bit longer to make sure the seafood is cooked.

5 tablespoons Kalaya House Curry Paste (page 55)

3 cups canned coconut milk

½ tablespoon shrimp paste

1 pound canned crabmeat (jumbo lump if you are feeling luxurious!) or chopped raw fish or shrimp

1 tablespoon light brown sugar

½ to 1 teaspoon kosher salt

2 tablespoons fish sauce

1 teaspoon freshly ground black pepper

2 red long hot chilies, thinly sliced on the diagonal

3 makrut lime leaves, torn

1 cup packed fresh basil leaves

1  In a blender or food processor, blend together the curry paste, 1 cup of the coconut milk, the shrimp paste, and ¼ cup of the canned crabmeat until very smooth.

2  In a medium pot or deep skillet, bring the mixture to a boil over high heat. When the liquid comes to a boil, pour in the remaining 2 cups coconut milk and stir until it comes back to a bubble. Stir in the brown sugar, salt, fish sauce, and black pepper and reduce the heat to low. Add the remaining crabmeat, chilies, lime leaves, and basil leaves. Stir until the basil leaves are wilted, then remove the pot from the heat. (If you're using raw fish or shrimp, cook for a minute or two longer to make sure they are cooked through.)

**Serve with:** Rice noodles or somen noodles, sliced raw cucumber, and raw or stir-fried long beans.

# CAENG SOM PAK TAI

## sour curry *with* shrimp & pineapple

SERVES 6

This is a fast, funky, and furious curry. If you have curry paste on hand, you simply add the ingredients and boil away! The essential sour taste, from tamarind, pineapple, and shrimp paste, cuts through heavier dishes on the Southern Thai table. Sour food opens up your appetite and makes you want to eat more.

My mother would drop a little MSG into this recipe, but you can just use bouillon. This recipe is true to the way we make it at home, but if you need to reduce the heat slightly, you can use less curry paste, and for a vegetarian version, swap the shrimp for mushrooms and the fish sauce for vegetarian fish sauce. My mom would serve this with salted fish, fried egg, and Thai black soy sauce. I love it with rice and a simple omelet.

There is a surprising and comforting sour funkiness to this curry, and it also pairs perfectly with the cold crunchiness of Khao Yum Kamin (page 104, Southern Thai Turmeric Rice Salad). You don't need to go to a yoga ashram to find balance—just step out of your comfort zone and embrace sour tastes.

I use unripe pineapple because it gives the dish a strong tang. If you use ripened pineapple, the flavor will be sweeter.

¾ cup Sour Curry Paste (page 50, Caeng Som)

1 tablespoon shrimp paste

1 tablespoon chicken or vegetarian bouillon powder

½ medium underripe (still firm) pineapple, peeled, quartered lengthwise, cored, and thinly sliced

¼ cup Thai Tamarind concentrate (see page 22)

2 tablespoons fish sauce

1½ to 2 teaspoons kosher salt

12 jumbo shrimp, peeled and deveined, tails left on

Juice of 1 lemon or 2 limes (about ¼ cup)

1   In a blender or food processor, combine the curry paste, shrimp paste, and 3¾ cups water and process until very smooth.

2   Pour the mixture into a wide pot or deep skillet. Set over high heat and bring to a boil. Stir in the bouillon powder, add the pineapple slices, reduce the heat to medium, and cook until the pineapple is tender and translucent, about 15 minutes.

3   Stir in the tamarind concentrate, fish sauce, and salt. Once this is combined, add the shrimp. When the liquid comes back to a bubble, turn off the heat and pour the lemon juice over top. Cover the pot and let it sit until the shrimp are just firm and opaque, about 5 minutes.

**Serve with:** Jasmine Rice (page 234) and my Khai Jiew Samoun Prai (page 249, Cilantro, Basil, and Scallion Omelet).

# PANANG CAI
## chicken panang curry

Let me be honest: Not all Panang curry is the same. In North America, it is often watered down and doesn't have much protein. But I won't let you be sad about this for too long, because my Panang curry will show off the lusciousness and spicy/herbal aroma it's meant to have, all with a moderate amount of heat.

Panang curry sets itself apart because of the toasty cumin and coriander, and paprika adds color and a mellow earthiness. I remember having to grind the spice myself when I was ten. If I could do it at ten years old, you can grind your own spices at home and make this quick and delicious curry, especially since you have your handy little spice grinder. I didn't have that when I was a kid!

Since there isn't a large amount of coconut cream in this recipe, you can avoid buying a can by skimming the cream off the top of a second can of coconut milk. Just make sure you put the can of coconut milk in the fridge first so the coconut cream hardens and you can see the difference between the cream and the milk.

2 tablespoons canola oil

5 tablespoons Red Curry Paste (page 52, Caeng Dang)

2 teaspoons paprika

3 tablespoons ground coriander, preferably ground from freshly toasted seeds (see page 18)

2 tablespoons ground cumin, preferably ground from freshly toasted seeds (see page 18)

2 tablespoons shrimp paste

2 cups canned coconut milk

2 pounds boneless, skinless chicken thighs and breasts, fat left on, cut into bite-size pieces

3 tablespoons light brown sugar

½ tablespoon freshly ground black pepper

2 tablespoons fish sauce

3 makrut lime leaves, torn

¼ cup plus 2 tablespoons coconut cream

1 or 2 red long hot chilies, thinly sliced on the diagonal

1 cup packed fresh basil leaves (stored in a bowl of cold water until ready to use)

1  In a medium pot or large deep skillet, combine the oil, curry paste, paprika, coriander, cumin, and shrimp paste. Set over medium-high heat and cook, stirring, until the shrimp paste has melted into the sauce. Reduce the heat to medium, pour in ½ cup of the coconut milk, and stir to create a smooth paste. When the curry bubbles and drops of oil separate on top, add the remaining coconut milk and stir it in with a whisk or wooden spoon. Let the curry bubble until the oil separates again, then add the chicken. Cook, stirring occasionally, until the chicken is just cooked through, 5 to 7 minutes.

2  Increase the heat to medium-high, scrape down the sides of the pot, and return to a boil. Let the curry bubble for a minute or two, then stir in the brown sugar and black pepper. Cook, stirring occasionally, until the sauce thickens, the oil separates into droplets on the top, and the color deepens a bit, 5 to 7 minutes. Stir in the fish sauce and lime leaves, then the coconut cream, chilies, and basil leaves. Remove from the heat and stir until the basil is wilted.

**Serve with:** Jasmine Rice (page 234) and stir-fried vegetables.

# NOK'S CHICKEN MASSAMAN CURRY
## gaeng massaman

SERVES 6 TO 8

You can read about the beautiful history of how massaman was brought to Malaysia and Thailand by Persian traders, and how the ingredients evolved as the dish traveled, but I am not your history teacher, I'm here to teach you how to cook. This dish is more personal for me. It's about the generations of market stall owners in Trang who still cook this dish and pass down their family recipe today. It's about how my house smelled when my mother made it, how rich the coconut cream used was, and how easy it is to make when you have the ingredients in your pantry. It can feed everyone in your family, including kids. My mom's massaman curry was so beloved that my uncle would come over to eat this sweet curry and then go to his dialysis appointment. My massaman curry, which contains warming star anise and cinnamon and comforting potatoes, develops a stronger depth of flavor the longer you cook it. Massaman is hearty and sweet as well as savory—just imagine the aroma in your house on a winter day as dinner bubbles on the stove and you sip a cup of tea.

Also, I never trim the chicken fat. Don't be afraid of fat. It adds heartiness to a dish.

8 cups coconut cream (about two 1-quart cartons or five 14-ounce cans)

1 cup Kalaya House Curry Paste (page 55)

2 tablespoons shrimp paste

4 tablespoons palm sugar or coconut sugar

¼ cup granulated sugar

2 pounds boneless, skinless chicken breast, cut into 1-inch cubes

4 star anise pods

2 cinnamon sticks

1 pound yellow onions, quartered and cut into thin wedges

1 pound russet potatoes, peeled and cut into 1-inch cubes

¾ cup unsalted roasted peanuts

¼ cup fish sauce

½ to 1 teaspoon kosher salt

½ teaspoon freshly ground black pepper

6 tablespoons tamarind concentrate (see page 22)

1   In a medium pot, bring 1 cup of the coconut cream to a simmer over medium heat. Stir in the curry paste, shrimp paste, and both sugars. Cook, stirring frequently to break up the palm sugar, until the paste is bubbling and fragrant, about 5 minutes.

2   Increase the heat to medium-high and stir in the remaining 7 cups of coconut cream, 1 cup at a time, letting the liquid come back to a bubble after each addition. Cook until the liquid thickens, 10 to 15 minutes.

3   Add the chicken, star anise, and cinnamon sticks. When the liquid returns to a boil, add the onions, potatoes, and peanuts. Bring back to a boil, reduce the heat to medium-low, and add the fish sauce, salt, and pepper. Cook, stirring occasionally, until the chicken is fully cooked and the potatoes are tender, 35 to 40 minutes.

4   Stir in the tamarind concentrate.

**Serve with:** Jasmine Rice (page 234).

# I'M JUST NOK

After you've finished shopping at the open-air market Talat Yan Ta Kow, walk down a quiet side street where the birds start to sound louder than the scooters, take a left turn at the orange-processing factory, and you will see a blanket of butterfly pea plants along a fence. Sprawling holy basil, lemongrass, and chili plants, with makrut lime trees reaching to the sky. Across the way is a two-story house, made in the old Trang architecture that mixes Chinese, Portuguese, and Malay styles, and looks to Americans a little like the houses of New Orleans.

I have come nine thousand miles from my home in Philadelphia to my mom's house, and I pause in front of the sweeping porch, airy entryway, and the abundance of plants nestled in containers along its sidewalk. Coming home is always exciting . . . and always a little stressful. Is my mom healthy? Is she happy? Is everyone in the family doing well? Being the big sister and the one who went abroad, I feel a sense of duty toward my family.

When I walk through the door I see the beautiful smiling face of my mom. She is sitting, waiting to greet me, wearing an orange and blue batik-print kaftan. She looks healthy and strong. Now in her seventies, she's retired, no longer making and selling her curry pastes at the market. She is so happy to see me.

She has spent decades of hard work at her curry paste stall and has been dedicated to feeding her family the best food using the freshest ingredients. Her devotion to her family, never thinking about what she would get in return, her generosity toward her customers, and her commitment to her work are qualities I carry with me today. It is her hope and determination that led me to leave Trang to go to one of the best schools in Bangkok, and then to look even beyond Thailand. For years, I explored the world as a first-class flight attendant, and that allowed me to have so many culinary experiences—and eventually develop my cooking style—but my mom's food will always be the best. The food I cook now reflects her influence on me. When I share my food with my customers in Philadelphia, I am sharing my mom's knowledge, passion, and love. But when I go home, I am not a famous chef and no one really knows the scale of my success. I'm just my mother's daughter. I'm just a big sister. I'm just Nok.

When I step into my mom's kitchen, I look at the two-burner stove hooked up to a gas tank, the stone mortar and pestle, and think about the market nearby, where I can buy any fresh ingredient I need to cook great food. In the United States, we invest in fancy, expensive chef's kitchens, but they won't make your food delicious. What you really need to cook good food is knowledge, good ingredients, and love.

I remember how Mom taught me how to pound the spices fine. She liked the toasted spices to be ground super fine, and I would grind them by hand, getting more and more tired, and she would tell me to keep going until the spices were perfect. But now, when I am stirring a big pot of curry made with fresh curry paste, it is like magic. I know when it's right by the aroma, the taste, and the color. It took years of watching and learning from my mom for me to know when it is just right.

I sometimes wish I could be at home more with her, but I have a lot of responsibilities in Philadelphia. I spoke to my mom on the phone while I was driving to my restaurant the other day, and she asked how many people were coming to my restaurant that night. I said three hundred. "Are you running a restaurant or a movie theater?" she asked.

I don't know if my family is proud of me, if they can understand just what I've achieved—how I command the kitchen, that the menu is about our traditions and transformation, and that the food I serve honors the story of my Southern Thai home. Do they know that little Nok who used to push the heavy cart of curry paste to the morning market is now an award-winning chef in America who shares her mother's food with the world? What would they think of the four giant Thai palm trees I've had installed in the middle of my restaurant, the custom-made chandeliers made by artists I love, which tell stories of gratitude and reflection? I do my best to visit every table, to make sure my customers are happy, and to radiate the kindness and generosity my mother taught me. My mom might never get to see it in person, but I always hope she knows she did good.

I first cooked for my mom when I had already moved to America; she had knee replacement surgery and I went back to visit. Finally, after all the times she made me chicken soup when I was sick or made sure that I ate my favorite foods when I was home from school, I got to cook for her.

I still learn from her; when I cook for her, we still share knowledge. But one day I was making tom hoi, her favorite clam soup. She watched me make it and said I put too much water in it. But when she tried it, she said it was really good.

Now, when I'm at home, she sometimes requests food she doesn't know how to cook, like dishes from Central Thailand, fermented pork with glass noodles and stinky beans, stir-fried pork liver, or even a different kind of nam prik, a chili dipping sauce, that she doesn't make herself. She asks me to make these things, and she sees that I am a good cook, too.

# GAENG KIEW WAAN OSSO BUCO
## green curry *with* beef shanks

You have never experienced a green curry like this. The gorgeous jungle-green color comes from basil, turmeric, and green curry paste and a last-minute addition of cilantro pureed in coconut milk.

As a chef, this is my favorite curry because it was a fun challenge to make the color a bright golden-green and beautiful, not murky.

Green curry can be sweet and spicy and herbaceous and work with so many proteins. What I love about this paired with beef shanks—which you can buy bone-in as osso buco in Italian markets—is how the braised meat nearly falls off the bone after cooking in the pot. For a quicker dish, you can skip the beef and make the same curry with shrimp—it's a dinner party favorite (just make the sauce starting from step 3, using a mix of coconut milk and water instead of the beef cooking liquid, and add about 1¾ pounds shrimp after the eggplants are tender in step 4, cooking just until they're done).

Also, hello, Pantone? Maybe next year the color of the year can be "Nok's Green Curry."

2½ pounds beef osso buco, cut into 3 pieces

4 cups canned coconut milk

1 cup Green Curry Paste (page 53, Gaeng Kiew Waan)

2 tablespoons shrimp paste

1 tablespoon ground turmeric

2 (70g) discs palm sugar or ½ cup brown sugar

3 Chinese eggplants, halved lengthwise and cut into 2-inch pieces

3 tablespoons fish sauce

½ to 1 teaspoon kosher salt

½ tablespoon freshly ground black pepper

½ tablespoon ground white pepper

1 cup packed fresh cilantro leaves

½ cup coconut cream

2 cups packed fresh basil leaves

5 makrut lime leaves, torn

15 green and red Thai chilies, smashed with the side of the knife

1   Put the osso buco in a Dutch oven or other large pot in a single layer. Pour in the coconut milk and 2 cups water. Bring to a boil over high heat, then reduce the heat to a gentle simmer and cook, uncovered, until the meat is very tender, about 4 hours.

2   Transfer the meat to a plate and pour the cooking liquid into a large measuring cup or heatproof bowl.

3   Return the pot to medium-high heat and add the curry paste, 1 cup of the cooking liquid, and the shrimp paste. Cook, stirring and breaking up the shrimp paste, until it melts into the sauce. Add the turmeric and cook until fragrant. Stir in the remaining cooking liquid and return the meat to the pot. When the liquid comes to a bubble, reduce the heat to medium-low, add the palm sugar, and cook, stirring occasionally, for 30 minutes.

4   Add the eggplant, pressing it down to submerge it as much as possible in the liquid, and increase the heat to high. Add the fish sauce, salt, black pepper, and white pepper and cook until the eggplant is tender and the meat shreds easily when you insert a fork, about 10 more minutes.

5   In a food processor or blender, puree the cilantro and coconut cream until very smooth.

6   Stir the basil into the curry until it is wilted, then stir in the cilantro/coconut cream mixture and turn off the heat. Stir in the lime leaves and Thai chilies.

**Serve with:** Jasmine Rice (page 234) or Green Coconut Rice (page 235).

# GAENG PAJARI
## seared tofu & pineapple coconut curry

Even though there are crisp-seared chunks of tofu here, it's the pineapple that is the star of this recipe, which will wow vegans and meat eaters alike. The fruit combines with my red curry sauce, a little bit of miso, and tofu to create a dish that is not overly sweet and has a delicate, balanced, nutty flavor. The pineapple has a surprisingly meaty texture and will be tender; cutting into it is like cutting into a piece of protein. This is often served as a side dish in Southern Thai Islamic cuisine and accompanies other, spicier curries.

Even though I said the pineapple is the star, be patient cooking the tofu. All sides of it have to be seared to a golden brown. This process is very important, and you cannot overcook tofu, so don't worry about that. (Well, unless you burn it, so you do have to pay *some* attention.) You don't need to drain the tofu on paper towels. If you sear the tofu well (and I know you will), the oil won't penetrate it.

4 tablespoons canola oil

1 tablespoon paprika

½ cup Red Curry Paste (page 52, Gaeng Dang)

1 tablespoon white miso

3¼ cups canned coconut milk

½ ripe pineapple, peeled (but not cored) and cut into 6 thick rounds

1 (14-ounce) package extra-firm tofu

1 tablespoon soy sauce

3 red long hot chilies, halved lengthwise, seeded, and cut into 2-inch pieces

4 or 5 makrut lime leaves, torn

1  In a wide, deep skillet or pot, heat 2 tablespoons of the oil over medium heat. Add the paprika and stir until it is fragrant; then add the curry paste and miso. Cook, stirring, until you can really smell the spices in the curry paste. Then stir in 1 cup of the coconut milk and increase the heat to high.

2  When the sauce begins to bubble, add the pineapple slices, arranging them in a single layer (it's fine if they overlap a little), then pour 2 cups of the coconut milk over top. This should fully submerge the pineapple slices; if it doesn't, pour in just enough water to submerge them (you shouldn't need much more than ½ cup). Reduce the heat to low and simmer until the pineapple cores are fork-tender and the oil has separated on the top of the sauce, 45 minutes to 1 hour, flipping the pineapple once halfway through.

3  When the pineapple has about 20 minutes left to cook, cut the tofu into 12 equal pieces (I like cubes, but you can do anything you want). Pat all the pieces dry with paper towels.

4  In large nonstick skillet, heat the remaining 2 tablespoons oil over high heat until just starting to smoke. Add the tofu in a single layer, reduce the heat to medium, and sear the tofu until it is golden brown on every side, about 10 minutes total. Put the seared tofu on a plate.

5  When the pineapple is finished cooking, add the soy sauce and tofu and stir gently to combine. Add the chilies and cook for a minute or two, until they soften a bit. Then add the lime leaves and cook for 1 or 2 more minutes, until fragrant. Finish with the remaining ¼ cup coconut milk, stirring it gently into the sauce.

6  Transfer the pineapple slices to a platter, top them with the tofu, and pour the sauce over top.

**Serve with:** Jasmine Rice (page 234).

# GAENG KUA GOONG LYCHEE

## red curry *with* prawns, cherry tomatoes & lychees

**SERVES 4 TO 6**

Forget about the clutter in your closet and let's be fancy!

In terms of cooking, this is still a quick weeknight dinner that is fun and easy. You sear the prawns for just a couple minutes until cooked; then you pour over a fast curry that is basically made by putting all the ingredients in a pot and bringing to a boil. Paprika gives the curry a beautiful red color, red curry paste gives it aroma and heat, dried shrimp gives it umami, and tomatoes and lychees make it sweet-tart. I love using river prawns because they have so much meat; in Thailand they are so large that people fish for them with fishing rods. And I love the drama: They inspire awe in dinner guests. They are my favorite thing to eat and they are becoming more widely available, usually frozen, but if you can't find river prawns, use jumbo shrimp and all will be well.

And for a refreshing summer treat, reserve the drained lychee juice and serve it over ice.

4 giant freshwater prawns (long feelers and legs removed), or 1 pound jumbo shrimp

¼ cup plus 2 tablespoons canola oil

1 tablespoon paprika

1 teaspoon shrimp paste

¼ cup Red Curry Paste (page 52, Gaeng Dang)

2 cups canned coconut milk

¼ cup Ground Dried Shrimp (page 137)

1 cup halved cherry tomatoes

1 (20-ounce) can lychees, drained (juice reserved to enjoy while you cook!)

1 tablespoon fish sauce

2 tablespoons tamarind concentrate (see page 22)

½ to 1 teaspoon kosher salt

1 tablespoon light brown sugar

Big pinch of freshly ground black pepper

2 red long hot chilies, thinly sliced, plus more for garnish

4 or 5 makrut lime leaves, torn, plus a few thinly sliced for garnish

1 cup packed fresh basil leaves, plus a few more, for garnish

1 Butterfly the prawns (or shrimp) with the shell on by cutting with a small, sharp knife along the underside almost all the way through from the head to the tail, then opening them up like a book. Clean out the eggs and other innards under running water and pat dry.

2 In a medium saucepan, heat 2 tablespoons of the oil over medium-high heat. Add the paprika and cook, stirring, until it is fragrant. Add the shrimp paste and curry paste and stir until the shrimp paste has melted. Stir in the coconut milk and ground dried shrimp.

3 Increase the heat to high, bring the liquid to a boil, and add the tomatoes. Wait until the liquid comes back to a boil, then add the lychees, fish sauce, tamarind concentrate, salt, brown sugar, and black pepper. Stir in the chilies, torn lime leaves, and basil and cook until the sauce comes back to a bubble. Turn off the heat.

4 In a large skillet, heat the remaining ¼ cup oil over medium heat. When the oil is hot, add the prawns, flesh-side up, in a single layer. Cook, using a spoon to baste the tops with oil, until the meat is opaque, about 5 minutes for giant prawns, 3 minutes for shrimp. Put the cooked prawns on a platter.

5 Spoon the sauce, tomatoes, and lychees over the prawns in the platter. Garnish with some thinly sliced chilies, thinly sliced lime leaves, and basil leaves.

**Serve with:** Jasmine Rice (page 234).

# KANG PAE
## spicy celebration goat curry

My father loved this very spicy dish. Goat curry is served at Islamic celebrations, house warmings, funerals, and weddings, and Thai people don't often cook this at home. Whenever my father heard this dish was being made in our community, he would seek it out and bring some to share with me.

I was excited to eat it with him and would wait for him to come home so we could eat the savory and bold curry together. Food can bring up memories and it can heal us, too. When I eat this, I don't feel sad about all the questions I didn't ask my father. It makes me feel close to him.

In Trang, goats are expensive. They don't sell goat meat by the pound, they have to butcher the goat whole, and the meat takes a while to cook because it has a lot of connective tissue. If you feel adventurous or want a pot bubbling on the stove for a long time, making your house smell amazing, try this recipe. Be brave, embrace new flavors, and keep making new memories.

7 cups canned coconut milk

1 goat or lamb leg (4 to 5 pounds), deboned and cut into 2-inch chunks (see Note)

1 cup Pepper Curry Paste (page 50, Caeng Kua Prig)

3 tablespoons shrimp paste

5 tablespoons Kruang Rah Spice (page 59) or garam masala

½ cup unsweetened coconut flakes

15 dried or fresh curry leaves

1 tablespoon freshly ground black pepper

1 tablespoon ground white pepper

1 tablespoon red chili flakes

5 or 6 makrut lime leaves, torn

1 In a large pot, combine 2 cups of the coconut milk and 5 cups water. Add the cubed goat meat, and if it is not fully submerged, pour in just enough water to cover it. Bring to a simmer over high heat; then reduce the heat to medium-low and cook for 1 hour. Do not let the liquid boil; reduce the heat as needed to keep it at a simmer.

2 When the goat has about 5 minutes of cooking left, in a medium pot or saucepan, combine the curry paste, shrimp paste, and 3 cups of the coconut milk and cook over medium-high heat. When the liquid begins to bubble, add the spice blend and cook, stirring, for 1 minute, until it's very fragrant.

3 After the goat has been simmering for 1 hour, increase the heat to high and bring to a boil. Pour in the coconut milk/curry paste mixture and reduce the heat again to medium-low to maintain a simmer. Simmer the curry until the meat is very tender, about 1 hour more.

4 Meanwhile, in a small dry skillet, toast the coconut flakes over low heat, stirring frequently, until it turns light golden, then caramel brown, about 5 minutes. (Trust me: You want a real brown color here. If you don't let it toast long enough, it won't grind to a powder as nicely.) Grind the toasted coconut in a mortar and pestle or spice grinder to a coarse powder, then keep grinding until it holds together when you pinch it with two fingers.

5 Once the goat is tender, stir in the coconut powder, curry leaves, black and white pepper, chili flakes, lime leaves, and the remaining 2 cups coconut milk. Bring to a bubble and turn off the heat.

**Serve with:** Jasmine Rice (page 234).

NOTE: Make friends with your butcher, they hold so much wisdom. Ask your butcher to get a goat leg for you and to debone and cube it, but be sure to keep the bone, too, because bone adds flavor. The sinew and the bones add a strong depth that lingers. For even more flavor, add the marrow and tendon to the curry.

# PAD PRIK KING HED

## dry red curry *with* pan-fried tofu & mushrooms

SERVES 4 TO 6

My mother is famous for this amazing vegan dish; the combination of mushroom and tofu is almost steak-like. If you are a meat eater, you will be surprised how satisfied you feel from this dish.

You will see the layers of flavor in this recipe; it's ginger-forward and umami-balanced because of the mushroom and miso. It's spicy with a hint of sweet. We use paprika to enhance the color and add a beautiful flavor. Mushrooms are not always common in the South, but we do have mushrooms that grow from rubber timber that grows in the mountains. It's not a saucy dish; it's more like the ingredients are coated in a super-flavorful paste.

Portobellos are easy to come by, but you could use fancy mushrooms from the farmers' market, too.

1 (14-ounce) package extra-firm tofu

2 tablespoons rice flour

Kosher salt and freshly ground black pepper

2 large portobello mushroom caps (about 10 ounces), cut into 2-inch chunks

7 tablespoons canola oil

¼ cup roughly chopped peeled fresh ginger (2 ounces)

¼ cup Red Curry Paste (page 52, Caeng Dang)

2 tablespoons paprika

2 tablespoons white miso

3 tablespoons light brown sugar

1 tablespoon soy sauce

½ pound long beans or green beans, trimmed and cut into 1-inch pieces

2 red long hot chilies, thinly sliced on the diagonal

½ teaspoon ground white pepper

5 makrut lime leaves, torn, plus sliced leaves for garnish

1  Drain the tofu, pat it dry with paper towels, and cut it into 1-inch cubes. In a small bowl, toss the cubed tofu with 1 tablespoon of the rice flour, a big pinch of salt, and a big pinch of black pepper.

2  Put the mushrooms in a large bowl and toss them with the remaining 1 tablespoon rice flour, a big pinch of salt, and a big pinch of black pepper.

3  In a large deep skillet or Dutch oven, heat 2 tablespoons of the oil over high heat until hot and just beginning to smoke. Add the mushrooms in a single layer and cook, stirring frequently, until the mushrooms are tender and browned on all sides, 5 to 7 minutes. Transfer the mushrooms to a plate, keeping the oil in the skillet.

4  In another large skillet, heat 2 tablespoons of the oil over high heat until just starting to smoke. Add the tofu in a single layer, reduce the heat to medium, and cook, turning occasionally, until the tofu is golden brown on every side, 8 to 10 minutes total. Transfer the seared tofu to a plate.

5  In a food processor or blender, puree the ginger, curry paste, and ½ cup water until smooth.

6  In the deep skillet with the mushroom oil, heat 2 more tablespoons of the oil over high heat. Pour in the curry paste mixture, the paprika, miso paste, and brown sugar. Stir well, mashing the miso into the other ingredients. When the sauce starts bubbling, add the mushrooms and tofu. Use two wooden spoons to mix everything together (you have two hands, so use them!).

7  Stir in the soy sauce, then add the long beans and remaining 1 tablespoon oil. Keep stirring with two spoons to coat everything. When the beans are just tender-crisp, after 3 to 5 minutes, add the chilies, 1 teaspoon black pepper, the white pepper, and the torn lime leaves.

**Serve with:** Jasmine Rice (page 234), garnished with thinly sliced lime leaves.

# HOR MOK MOO

## steamed pork & crabmeat curry

MAKES 6 SERVINGS

The technique of steaming meats may challenge what you think you know about curry, but that's what I'm here for. The final dish comes out like a cross between a custard and a soufflé, fragrant with yellow curry paste, lemongrass, makrut lime, and the briny taste of ground shrimp flavoring the pork and crab. In Thailand, we make the mixture in a big clay pot and keep stirring until it gets very thick. Then we steam the mixture in a banana leaf. Here, it's as simple as stirring together the mixture, putting it into ramekins, and steaming it. It comes out rich and decadent, and it's delicious with rice, other curries, and sweet stir-fries like Moo Hong (page 228, Braised Pork Belly). There is no better way to say "I'm thinking of you," when you present your guests and family with their own super-cute ramekin filled with hor mok moo.

2 large eggs

1½ cups canned coconut milk

1 tablespoon Ground Dried Shrimp (recipe follows)

3 tablespoons Kalaya House Curry Paste (page 55)

5 tablespoons fish sauce

2 tablespoons plus 2 teaspoons rice flour

5 tablespoons light brown sugar

2 to 3 teaspoons kosher salt, plus more for the sauce

1 pound ground pork

½ pound canned jumbo lump crabmeat

6 or 7 makrut lime leaves, very thinly sliced

1 red long hot, thinly sliced

18 large basil leaves

### FOR GARNISH

1 red long hot, thinly sliced on the diagonal

2 or 3 makrut lime leaves, very thinly sliced

Basil leaves

1  To set up a steamer, pour 1 to 2 inches of water into a large deep skillet or pot. If you have a large steamer rack that fits, set it in the skillet or pot now. If you have a large metal or bamboo steamer basket, have it nearby. Arrange six 6-ounce heatproof bowls or ramekins on the steamer rack or in your steamer basket to make sure they will all fit. (If not, you will have to work in batches.)

2  Crack the eggs into a large bowl. Pour in 1 cup of the coconut milk, the ground dried shrimp, curry paste, fish sauce, 2 tablespoons of the rice flour, the brown sugar, and salt. Whisk everything together until smooth. Add the ground pork and mix with your hand until it is fully incorporated. Gently mix in all but ¼ cup of the crabmeat, the thinly sliced lime leaves, and all but 6 slices of the red chili.

3  Put the steamer skillet or pot over high heat.

4  Line the bottom of each ramekin with 3 large basil leaves. Divide the meat mixture among the ramekins and smooth the tops. Press 3 or 4 pieces of the reserved lump crabmeat and 1 slice of red chili into the top of each ramekin.

5  When the water in the steamer is simmering, arrange the ramekins directly on the rack or in the steamer basket, cover with a lid, and steam until the internal temperature of the ground pork mixture registers between 145° and 160°F on an instant-read thermometer, about 20 minutes. (The curry will be smoother and more delicate at the lower temperature, but some people want their pork *very* cooked.)

6  In a small saucepan, combine the remaining ½ cup coconut milk, 2 teaspoons rice flour, and a big pinch of salt. Whisk over low heat until the mixture is very thick, 2 to 3 minutes. Increase the heat to high and cook, whisking constantly, for about 20 seconds. Remove the pan from the heat.

7  Serve with the coconut milk sauce on top and a garnish of sliced chilies, lime leaves, and basil leaves.

## ground dried shrimp
### MAKES ABOUT ¾ CUP

Having ground dried shrimp prepped in advance really helps recipes come together quickly. In Thai cooking, ground dried shrimp adds texture and umami. Don't skip this ingredient, as it really makes a difference in the flavor.

1 (3-ounce) package dried shrimp

In a food processor, pulse the dried shrimp until finely ground (the texture of finely grated Parmesan cheese). Store the ground dried shrimp in an airtight container in the refrigerator. It will keep for up to 1 month.

# CHUCHEE HOI SHELL

## dinner-party seared scallops & crabmeat in yellow curry sauce

**SERVES 6**

This recipe was my number-one bestseller at my first restaurant, and you will be amazed at how simple it is to put together: You stir together the curry ingredients and just bring to a simmer, then cook some scallops in a hot pan, and you're done. The crab and scallops are so meaty and appetizing, and the deep orange from yellow curry paste and coconut milk reminds me of sunset. This is an elegant weeknight curry or an effortless dinner-party dish. It doesn't require a lot of thought, just ingredients you have in your pantry and my Kalaya curry paste. Scallops cook so quickly, you can finish this recipe in minutes. That means you'll have time to cook your other favorite recipes like Hoi Mang Phu Ob Samun Prai (page 227, Baked Mussels with Herbs) and share a true Southern Thai feast!

1½ cups plus 2 tablespoons canned coconut milk

3 tablespoons Kalaya House Curry Paste (page 55)

½ tablespoon shrimp paste

1 tablespoon Ground Dried Shrimp (page 137)

2 tablespoons light brown sugar

1 teaspoon plus 1 pinch ground white pepper

½ teaspoon freshly ground black pepper

1 tablespoon fish sauce

5 or 6 makrut lime leaves, torn

½ cup packed (about 4 ounces) jumbo lump crabmeat

1 pound large dry-packed scallops (U10) (see Note)

Kosher salt

2 teaspoons rice flour

2 tablespoons canola oil

**FOR GARNISH**

Thinly sliced makrut lime leaves

1 red long hot, very thinly sliced on the diagonal

15 to 20 pieces jumbo lump crabmeat

1  In a medium pot, combine ½ cup of the coconut milk, the curry paste, shrimp paste, and ground dried shrimp and cook over medium heat, stirring and breaking up the shrimp paste with a wooden spoon, until the mixture is aromatic and oil begins to separate on top, 1 to 2 minutes. Increase the heat to high and cook, stirring, for 20 more seconds to intensify the flavors.

2  Pour in the remaining 1 cup plus 2 tablespoons of the coconut milk, the brown sugar, 1 teaspoon of the white pepper, the black pepper, fish sauce, lime leaves, and crabmeat. Let the mixture come to a bubble, then reduce the heat to low to keep the curry warm while you cook the scallops.

3  Put the scallops in a bowl. Pat them dry. Add a pinch of salt, a pinch of white pepper, and the rice flour. Toss until coated.

4  In a large skillet, heat the oil over high heat until it begins to smoke. Add the scallops and cook just until they are opaque in the center and golden brown on the outside, 1 to 2 minutes per side.

5  Pour the curry into a serving bowl, nestle the scallops on top, and garnish with thinly sliced lime leaves, sliced chili, and more crabmeat.

NOTE: When buying scallops, I always buy "dry" ones—not "dried," like the hard scallops in Asian markets, but "dry-packed," meaning scallops that have not been treated by a chemical that makes them absorb flavorless water (called "wet-packed"). They will be more expensive, but the quality is worth it.

# KANG KUA PRIK KRA DOUK MOO
## simple southern water-based curry *with* spareribs

**SERVES 4 TO 6**

Sour, spice, funk, salt, and sea! When I was a flight attendant, I always missed this simple water-based curry. I would put it on a list for my mother to cook because its complexity is in the reduction, which makes it savory and rich. I like it with bone-in ribs because it's more flavorful. You find it on almost every Southern table; it's part of our daily curry spread.

The saltiness comes from shrimp paste and fish sauce, lime leaves come from the garden outside, and spareribs are always delicious. Having my curry paste in the freezer means you can get this dish out in under 45 minutes and have a beautiful bubbling pot on the stove. Enjoy this curry. Embrace the funk.

Remember, this curry is better the next day; when you keep reducing it down, the flavors will become even more complex and vibrant.

2 pounds bone-in pork spareribs, cut into 2-inch pieces (ask your butcher to do this)

Handful of kosher salt

3 tablespoons shrimp paste

½ cup Pepper Curry Paste (page 50, Caeng Kua Prig)

1 tablespoon freshly ground black pepper

1 tablespoon ground white pepper

1 tablespoon fish sauce

5 or 6 makrut lime leaves, torn

1 Put the pork ribs in a large pot, cover them with cold water, and toss in a handful of salt. Bring to a boil over high heat, then drain the pork in a colander and rinse it thoroughly under cold running water. This makes sure that the curry is clean of scum (so you don't have to skim the top).

2 Meanwhile, in a large pot, combine 7 cups water, the shrimp paste, and curry paste and bring to a boil over high heat. Reduce the heat to medium and add the pork. Cook until the pork is tender, about 45 minutes.

3 Stir in the black pepper, white pepper, fish sauce, and lime leaves.

**Serve with:** Jasmine Rice (page 234), Moo Waan (page 175, My Mother's Caramelized Pork), and crunchy vegetables.

# TOM

**Soup is the universe in one pot. It is a way of saying "I love you," without having to say it out loud.**

Soup can be something you eat when you are sick or feeling cold, or with the right spices it can cool you down on a hot day. There is a universal comfort in soup and in the process of making soup. It preserves the nutrition of ingredients that might be thrown out, like bones and organs—and they carry a deep rich flavor. It's about having an easy meal—even if the ingredients list seems long, most of the recipes here don't require much more work than putting everything in a pot and boiling for a few minutes. It's about the way your house smells, and the way you feel when having soup.

In Thailand, soup can be a meal in itself—like stopping at an outdoor soup stall that serves a big bowl of rice noodles, broth, and a drumstick for lunch—or it can be part of a broader meal and act as a palate cleanser between bites, or make you want to eat more. It is balancing and joyful. You might be thinking, "Thailand is hot, and soup is for winter!" But in Thailand it's part of our everyday table all year long. There is a belief in many parts of Asia that if you eat hot soup in hot weather, it will cool you down, but I say it's about enjoying a range of flavor. Soup helps you pause and stay in the present. When you eat something spicy, you just sip soup from the spoon and then get back to the rest of the food. When a bowl of soup is a full meal like at a food stall, it features protein, noodles, and vegetables and you get all your food groups and feel nourished. There is nothing better than when you can share a soup you made, or someone makes you a bowl of soup when you are having a bad day.

You may find some of the soup flavors in this chapter new and exciting, like Soup Hang Wua (page 157, Oxtail Soup with Herbs and Crispy Shallots), which is infused with aromatics, or Tom Hoi (page 153, My Mother's Umami-Packed Clam Soup). And you will also find them deeply familiar, like the bright, spicy Tom Yum Goong (page 150, Hot and Sour Thai Soup with Shrimp). If you're reading this book, you must have had tom yum a hundred times, right? That tom yum was probably made with a store-bought mix with a few cherry tomatoes and three little shrimp. I don't blame anyone, everyone needs to make a living. But when you try my recipe, with homemade shrimp stock and chili jam, fresh makrut lime leaves, and galangal, you will wonder where I've been all your life.

And there's Gai Tom Kamin (page 149, My Mother's Turmeric Chicken Soup for a Cold), because almost no matter where you reside in the world, chicken soup is something that connects us all.

In tough times, soup is about making ingredients go a long way and taking a respectful no-waste approach to our food. And in good times, soup is about drawing out a new type of flavor from leftover shells, bones, or meats that might otherwise be thrown out. This is also how you can develop your flavor of hand, each soup

you make might be slightly different as you find different ingredients and styles that suit you. Soup can be sophisticated or simple—it really just depends on how you feel that day.

I am so happy to share these recipes with you, and I hope they become mainstays in your kitchen that your kids and your family will remember. In hard times you make soup, in good times you make soup, and no matter what life brings you, soup helps you keep going on.

# NAM SOUP GAI
## chicken broth

MAKES ABOUT 7 QUARTS

This is a simple stock that is the base of so many things. It's delicious but not overly rich; it will take on flavor beautifully and not overpower anything.

You might notice that I don't tell you to skim the fat from the top of the pot. It doesn't make you a bad person if you skim, but you may lose some important flavor. Relax, chill, and decide for yourself.

1 whole chicken or, ideally, stewing hen (about 3 pounds)

2 large yellow onions, peeled and cut in half

10 large garlic cloves, peeled but whole

Handful of fresh cilantro sprigs

1 large carrot, peeled and chopped into 3 pieces

1   Rinse the chicken thoroughly and carefully so as not to splash the water out of the sink, inside and out, then put the whole thing (including the gizzards) in a very large stockpot. Add 8 quarts water, the onions, garlic, cilantro, and carrot. Bring to a boil over high heat, then reduce the heat to low and simmer for 3 hours. Do not allow the broth to boil. (You won't need to skim anything off the top if you rinse the chicken really well.)

2   Remove the chicken from the broth. (I let it cool and then shred the meat to use in chicken salad.) Strain out the vegetables and discard. Also discard the carcass if you've pulled the meat off. Let the broth cool and store in the refrigerator in an airtight container for up to 5 days, or freeze for longer.

# SHRIMP SHELL STOCK

MAKES ABOUT 4½ CUPS

Why are Americans afraid of shells? These are flavor bombs that add depth and umami to your stock. Don't be afraid! Buy shell-on or even better, head-on and shell-on shrimp, peel them, and save the shells in a thick plastic bag in the freezer until you get enough shells to make stock. This is amazing to have on hand for Tom Yum Goong (page 150, Hot and Sour Thai Soup with Shrimp).

Shells from 1 pound shrimp

¼ cup thinly sliced galangal (about 2 ounces)

Handful of cilantro stems, smashed

1 large shallot, halved, peeled, and smashed

5 garlic cloves, smashed

1 stalk fresh or frozen lemongrass, smashed and tied in a knot

¼ yellow onion, peeled and cut into 1-inch pieces

4 makrut lime leaves, bruised and torn

Stems from 1 (8-ounce) package white mushrooms

In a stockpot, combine the shells and 8 cups water. Bring to a bubble over high heat, then add the galangal, cilantro, shallot, garlic, lemongrass, onion, lime leaves, and mushroom stems. Reduce the heat to medium-low and simmer for 30 minutes. Strain the stock, let cool, and store in the refrigerator in an airtight container for up to 5 days, or freeze for longer.

# GAI TOM KAMIN

## my mother's turmeric chicken soup for a cold

SERVES 4 TO 6

When I was a little girl and feeling sick . . . I remember how my mother would make this for me. There is something so special when someone else makes chicken soup for you. When you grow up, you have to take care of yourself, and you realize you are on your own and miss that love and care. When I moved to America, in the wintertime I made this soup for myself to warm up and remind me of my home. It's earthy yellow and vibrant from the turmeric, which adds beautiful mellow flavor and that color, and helps boost your immunity. Thai chicken soup uses cilantro instead of parsley, and I use shallots instead of onion because that's what my mother used. The aromatics of garlic, cilantro, and shallots will make your house smell inviting, and it will heal your heart and restore your soul. Plus, you have to smash the lemongrass. Smashing is therapeutic to get that tension out, another way to heal your heart and restore your soul.

Handful of fresh cilantro stems and leaves

1 large shallot or 1 small red or yellow onion, peeled and cut into small wedges

¼ cup garlic cloves, smashed

2 fresh lemongrass stalks (optional), both ends trimmed off, smashed with a pestle or the smooth end of a meat mallet

2 scallions, both ends trimmed off, smashed with a pestle or the smooth end of a meat mallet

½ tablespoon freshly ground black pepper

½ tablespoon ground white pepper

1½ to 2 tablespoons kosher salt

2 bone-in, skin-on chicken thighs and 2 chicken legs

1 tablespoon ground turmeric

3 tablespoons fish sauce

2 tablespoons sugar

### FOR SERVING

Glass noodles (cooked according to the package directions) or Jasmine Rice (page 234)

Fresh cilantro leaves

Fried Shallots, homemade (page 45) or store-bought

Thinly sliced Thai chilies or red long hot chilies

Thinly sliced scallions

Lime wedges, for squeezing

1  In a large pot, combine 12 cups water, the cilantro, shallot, garlic, lemongrass (if using), scallions, black pepper, white pepper, salt, and chicken. Add the turmeric to kick your germs away. Bring to a boil over high heat. Then reduce the heat to medium-low and simmer until the chicken is tender and the broth is flavorful, about 30 minutes.

2  Remove from the heat and stir in the fish sauce and sugar.

3  Serve hot on its own or with glass noodles or rice, topped with cilantro, fried shallots, thinly sliced chilies and scallions, and lime wedges for squeezing.

# TOM YUM GOONG

## hot & sour thai soup *with* shrimp

SERVES 4 TO 6

The tom yum goong at my restaurant is spectacular. When it comes out, it is visually stunning, with giant river prawns hanging over the edge of a heated hot pot. It is a piece of art and everyone says "Wow!"

The tom yum goong we cook at home is just as delicious—spicy, sour, herbal, fresh, and tasting deeply of shrimp—even if the presentation is more humble. This is a fast and casual weeknight meal and when they taste it, everyone will say "Wow!"

If you didn't take my advice and save your shrimp shells to make Shrimp Shell Stock (page 146), it's okay, I'm not mad. You can use your favorite chicken or seafood stock, then infuse it over medium-low heat with the aromatics from the shrimp stock recipe for 15 minutes.

4 cups Shrimp Shell Stock (page 146)

1 small yellow onion, cut into 1-inch cubes

5 thick slices galangal (see Note)

1 large shallot, chopped

¼ cup fish sauce

1 tablespoon light brown sugar

1½ to 2 teaspoons kosher salt

1 cup halved cherry tomatoes

1 (8-ounce) package white button mushrooms, stemmed and quartered

5 garlic cloves, finely chopped

15 to 20 Thai chilies, smashed

2 tablespoons Mom's Chili Jam (page 257, Nam Prik Phao)

1 pound jumbo shrimp, peeled and deveined, tails removed

½ cup fresh lime juice (about 4 limes)

3 scallions, cut into ½-inch pieces

½ cup chopped fresh cilantro

5 makrut lime leaves, torn

1   In a medium saucepan or pot, bring the shrimp stock to a simmer over medium heat. Add the onion, galangal, and shallot. Increase the heat to high and bring to a boil, then stir in the fish sauce, brown sugar, salt, tomatoes, mushrooms, garlic, and chilies.

2   Pour a ladle of broth into a small bowl, add the chili jam, and whisk until smooth. Add this mixture back to the pot. Stir, then add the shrimp. Pour in the lime juice and stir in the scallions, cilantro, and lime leaves. Cook just until the shrimp are opaque and firm, 2 to 3 minutes.

3   Take off the heat and serve.

NOTE: Fresh galangal is very hard to find in the United States. Look for it frozen in the Asian market, where the quality is consistent.

# TOM HOI
## my mother's umami-packed clam soup

**SERVES 4 TO 6**

When you make this soup you will be happy as a clam, and happiness comes quick, because it's done in 10 minutes once you get the water boiling. This is such a quick-cooking soup, the clams have a good briny flavor, and lemongrass and basil add a brightness to the garlic, shallots, and chilies and make it stand out. Remember, umami is a feeling, not just a taste, and this soup brings forth that state of mind. In Trang, the fisherman would bring the clams from a nearby village and my mom would clean them and make this when everything was at peak freshness.

50 Manila clams
(3 pounds)

1 lemongrass stalk, trimmed, cut into 2-inch pieces, and smashed with a knife or the smooth side of a meat mallet

3 large shallots, peeled and smashed

10 garlic cloves, smashed

2 to 3 teaspoons kosher salt

1 teaspoon chicken bouillon powder

½ teaspoon freshly ground black pepper

½ teaspoon ground white pepper

1 cup packed fresh basil leaves

8 to 10 green Thai chilies, smashed with the side of a large knife

Jasmine Rice (page 234), for serving

1   Soak the clams in a large bowl of cold water to allow them to purge any sand. Your clams might also need scrubbing. Take a look at the bottom of the bowl after about 10 minutes; if there is visible dirt, remove the clams, rinse or scrub them, and soak again, until there is no sand. I know I said this is a quick soup, but sometimes you get unlucky and you get very sandy clams. Drain and rinse them really well.

2   In a large pot, bring 10 cups water to a boil over high heat. Add the lemongrass, shallots, garlic, and salt. When the water comes to a boil, add the clams. Let it come back to a boil, then reduce the heat to medium and cook just until the clams open, about 7 minutes, but keep an eye on them because once they open, they are done. Cooking them longer will make them rubbery.

3   Add the bouillon powder, black pepper, and white pepper. Stir in the basil and Thai chilies. Serve with rice.

# KANG JUED WOON SEN

## pork meatball soup & glass noodles *with* fried garlic oil

**SERVES 4 TO 6**

I don't remember playing so much when I was a kid, but I *do* remember eating. This is the soup that every kid will enjoy. *Jued* means "light flavor," and this is a mild gentle soup that is still complex in its taste. The glass noodles give a beautiful bouncy chew, the pork is like a meatball, the tofu offers a nice soft protein, and the chicken broth is so cozy. You can make the meatballs first and freeze them until you want to make the soup. It's okay to be a kid again sometimes!

**PORK MEATBALLS**

4 large garlic cloves, coarsely chopped

1 tablespoon finely chopped cilantro stems

2 scallions, very thinly sliced

½ pound ground pork

1 tablespoon fish sauce

1 teaspoon light brown sugar

Big pinch of ground white pepper

Big pinch of freshly ground black pepper

**SOUP**

4 ounces uncooked glass noodles

6 cups Chicken Broth (page 146, Nam Soup Gai) or store-bought, or water

2 tablespoons fish sauce

½ to 1 teaspoon kosher salt

1 teaspoon light brown sugar

½ tablespoon sesame oil

6 scallions, cut into 2-inch pieces

2 stalks Chinese celery, trimmed and cut into ½-inch pieces (see Note)

1 tablespoon chopped fresh cilantro

1 (16-ounce) package silken tofu, drained and cut into large cubes

¼ cup Garlic Oil (page 45), for serving

Fried Garlic (page 45), for serving

1. **Prepare the pork:** On a cutting board, chop the garlic, cilantro, and scallions together until they are minced. Put the aromatics in a bowl and add the ground pork. Mix with your hand until everything is evenly distributed; then add the fish sauce, brown sugar, white pepper, and black pepper. Mix well. Cover and refrigerate for 30 minutes or up to overnight.

2. **Make the soup:** Soak the glass noodles in cold water for 10 minutes, or according to the package directions. Drain well, cut the noodles in half with kitchen shears, and set aside.

3. Pour the chicken broth into a medium pot and set over high heat. Roll the pork mixture into tablespoon-size balls and drop them into the broth. When the broth begins to boil, add the fish sauce, salt, brown sugar, and sesame oil. Stir in the glass noodles and bring back to a boil. Stir in the scallions, Chinese celery, and cilantro. Finally, drop the tofu into the soup, stir gently until the tofu is hot, and serve.

4. Top each serving with some garlic oil and fried garlic.

**NOTE:** Chinese celery is much thinner and stronger than typical American celery. If you can't find it, use ½ cup of chopped leaves from a bunch of standard celery.

# SOUP HANG WUA
## nok's childhood oxtail soup *with* herbs & crispy shallots

SERVES 6

My mother put every type of meat and vegetable on the table and it was always good.

I learned to appreciate the beauty of a good cut of meat from an early age. Oxtail is so special and so delicious. It adds so much creaminess and depth to the soup because of its gelatin and this soup is a clean bite that can be paired with other dishes on a cool day. In Trang, this dish is served alongside a chicken biryani (page 69, Khao Mok Ghai), and I recommend you freeze any extra broth and pair it with glass noodles for an extra meal.

This is a recipe you let simmer so you can do the things you love and still take care of people. Serve your kids this soup so they grow up sophisticated and learn the joy of trying everything on the table.

6 pounds bone-in oxtail

½ cup garlic cloves, peeled but whole

1½ cups chopped or thinly sliced peeled galangal (6 ounces), fresh or thawed if frozen

5 medium shallots (7 ounces), peeled, halved, and smashed with the side of a knife

2 lemongrass stalks, trimmed, outer leaves removed, rinsed well, tied together in a knot

Stems from 1 bunch cilantro

5 makrut lime leaves

¼ cup rock sugar (see Note)

2 medium yellow onions, quartered, cut into ½-inch-thick wedges

1 pint cherry tomatoes or grape tomatoes, halved

2 to 3 tablespoons kosher salt

4 tablespoons fish sauce

### FOR GARNISH

12 Thai red chilies

6 garlic cloves, peeled but whole

Leaves from 1 bunch cilantro

2 limes, cut into wedges

Fried Shallots (page 45)

Fish sauce, for serving

1   Place the oxtails in a large pot and pour in enough water to fully cover them. Bring the water to a boil over high heat, then turn off the heat. Drain the oxtails and transfer them to a large bowl of cold water. Let the oxtail soak while you prepare the aromatics and broth. (This helps keep the broth clear and less greasy.) Rinse out the pot.

2   Crush the garlic and galangal with a mortar and pestle, just until you can smell them.

3   In the same large pot you used to boil the oxtail, combine 6 quarts water, the garlic, galangal, shallots, lemongrass, cilantro stems, lime leaves, and rock sugar. Transfer the oxtail to the pot. Bring to a boil over high heat, then reduce the heat to a simmer. Cook until the oxtail meat is very tender, 2 to 2½ hours, skimming the foam off the top. You'll know it's done when a paring knife can go easily in the meat without resistance.

4   Add the onions to the pot and increase the heat to high. When the broth comes to a boil, add the tomatoes. Reduce the heat to low and simmer until the onions are translucent, for about 15 minutes, skimming fat off the top every few minutes. Stir in the salt and fish sauce.

5   When you're ready to serve, prepare the garnishes: Smash the Thai chilies and garlic cloves with the side of a large knife, and place 2 chilies and 1 garlic clove in each of six soup bowls. Chop the cilantro leaves and divide them among the bowls, reserving a small handful for the top of each bowl. Squeeze the juice of 1 lime wedge into each bowl.

6   Using tongs, divide the oxtail among the bowls. Ladle the broth over top, and make sure each bowl gets some onion and tomato, too. Sprinkle with fried shallots and finish each bowl with a splash of fish sauce and some fresh cilantro leaves.

NOTE: If you don't have rock sugar, you can use a mix of 4 teaspoons granulated sugar and 4 teaspoons brown sugar, but I recommend the gentle flavor of rock sugar.

# PAD & THOD

**Stir-fry is what you make when you come home from work and can't decide what to cook yet still hope to make a beautiful meal.**

It's fast, it's delicious, and it features proteins and vegetables as well as aromatics, pastes, and spices. A stir-fry can be a one-plate meal or one of many dishes on the Southern Thai table. They are so quick and easy you could make a few stir-fries at once with some ambition and planning, and ingredients can be subbed with whatever you have if you are in a jam.

So here is the most important secret for great stir-fry: For a stir-fry to taste and feel the way it should, your wok has to be smoking hot. So hot you are a little afraid you will set off the fire alarm. So hot you fear your neighbor will call to make sure everything is okay. Just when you think it's hot enough, pause. Wait some more. Then wait a little more. And then you can begin to cook. American stove burners do not offer the same amount of heat as those in Thailand, so you need to maximize the heat in the pan. Stir-fries need to be cooked quickly and over a heat that will help promote caramelization.

To truly know when the wok is ready, you should see light wisps of smoke coming off it, and oil added and swirled around this wok should immediately be shimmering-hot and start to smoke a little as well. (If your oil starts billowing smoke, okay, you've actually gotten it too hot. Don't cook with it, turn off the flame, pour it out into a heatproof bowl, and discard it when cool. And start the pan over.)

When you're done, you want to see beautifully cooked vegetables and bites of meat with their distinctive flavor, ideally with little spots of browning or even a little char. The vegetables in a stir-fry should be firm, the proteins just-cooked, and the spices and aromatics should not burn. (Never put your garlic in first, please!!!)

Cooking was my mom's work and it was her life. She never tired of cooking for us, even after a long day. My mom cooked through instinct based on what was available in the market. She picked the best ingredients, and her prep would be minimal; we had the pastes and sauces ready from the day. Since you don't have your own curry stall, it's a good idea to prep some of the curry pastes and sauces beforehand or have them frozen and ready to go. Don't forget to make a pot of rice as you are prepping and cooking, as it goes well with all of these recipes and can be an easy one-plate meal.

As you are cooking these recipes, you will learn to feel confident at the helm of a smoking skillet. If you have had my Turmeric Fish (page 163, Pla Kamin), My Mother's Caramelized Pork (page 175, Moo Waan), Stir-Fried Crab in Curry Powder Sauce (page 168, Poo Pad Pong Karee), or Pickled Mustard Greens with Eggs (page 183, Pad Pak Kad Dong), at my restaurant, you can re-create those flavors at home with grace and ease. If you have never tried any of these recipes, they will open your world and make you think about how good dinner can be. You will make your own kitchen memories as the sound of aromatics hitting a hot, smoking wok connects cooks to all of the generations before.

The sizzles and pops awaken the spirit of your ancestors and your heart.

All of these recipes pair well with rice, so make your pot of rice and get cooking, and to impress your friends with little effort, just add an omelet (see page 249). The recipes in this chapter are balanced, flavorful, and delicious, and once you master them, you can prepare dinner any day in less than 30 minutes with a little prep. So good, so fast, so efficient, so done.

# PLA KAMIN

## turmeric fish

**SERVES 6**

After school, I used to rush home to help my mom prepare her curry pastes for the next day. I would painstakingly peel turmeric roots one by one. My small hands would stain yellow as we peeled kilo after kilo to prepare for making the paste. To this day I am not a big fan of peeling turmeric—I have no special tricks even after years of experience. It can be hard work, but the color and flavor of fresh turmeric are so rewarding and cannot be replaced.

In Southern Thai cuisine, a number of dishes use fresh turmeric root as the main ingredient. The turmeric paste can be used as a marinade for any protein. Turmeric makes the fish in this dish an earthy gold color, and the flavor is sweet and mellow. You marinate the fish in the paste and a touch of sugar, then quickly sear it in oil with fresh garlic and fish sauce. Once you have the fresh turmeric paste ready, which I recommend you do and keep in the fridge, turmeric fish is quick and easy to prepare, making it ideal for family meals.

2 pounds monkfish fillets, cut into ½-inch-thick medallions

¾ cup Turmeric Paste (page 55)

1 tablespoon light brown sugar

½ to 1 teaspoon kosher salt

5 tablespoons fish sauce

½ cup vegetable oil

7 large garlic cloves, roughly chopped

1 tablespoon freshly ground black pepper

1 teaspoon ground white pepper

Jasmine Rice (page 234), for serving

1   In a large bowl, gently mix the monkfish pieces with the turmeric paste, brown sugar, salt, and 3 tablespoons of the fish sauce until they are evenly coated.

2   Set a wok over high heat and let it heat up until it begins to smoke. Add the vegetable oil and let it heat up until it is restless in the pan and just begins to smoke. Immediately add the fish pieces to the hot oil and use two wooden or silicone spatulas to spread them out in a single layer. Scatter the garlic on top of the fish, then sprinkle with the black pepper and white pepper. Grab the two spatulas again and use them to mix the fish just like you would toss a big salad, scooping along the bottom of the wok from the sides toward the middle, rotating until the pepper and garlic are evenly distributed.

3   Rearrange the fish in a single layer and let cook undisturbed for 2 minutes. Use the spatulas—and the same salad-tossing motion—to flip the fish. Make sure the pieces are spread out in a single layer again, and cook for 1 minute without stirring.

4   Drizzle the remaining 2 tablespoons fish sauce around the edges of the wok. The fish should be cooked through at this point. Remove the wok from the heat.

5   Serve with steamed rice.

# MOO KAPI
## stir-fried pork in shrimp paste

SERVES 4

Moo kapi is a good example of Peranakan cuisine—a blend of Chinese, Malay, and Indonesian cooking styles—and is a reflection of how many unique communities immigrated to Southern Thailand. When I make this, I remember how my mom always wrapped shrimp paste in banana leaves and grilled them lightly, the traditional Southern Thai way of mellowing the aroma of the pungent ingredient. You shouldn't be afraid of the shrimp paste, because it adds a delicious umami-sweetness to a recipe and its flavor gets better as it's cooked.

The flavor of this dish is a showstopper. The sauce for the pork is fatty and comforting and tangy-sweet, with heat from the chilies and a balance of umami from fish sauce and the citrus of the lime juice. Cooking the star ingredient, the shrimp paste, rounds out its pungent flavor while keeping its fermented depth. The baking soda will keep the pork tender even after cooking. No one wants tough pork.

The list of ingredients looks long on this one, but the cook time is again quick—the stir-frying takes just a few minutes. Remember, this pork is meant to be glossy and beautiful.

### MARINATED PORK

1½ pounds pork tenderloin, cut into ¼-inch-thick slices

¼ cup vegetable oil

¼ cup fish sauce

2 to 3 teaspoons kosher salt

2 tablespoons granulated sugar or light brown sugar

1 teaspoon baking soda

1 teaspoon freshly ground black pepper

1 teaspoon ground white pepper

### STIR-FRY

½ cup vegetable oil

1 small white onion, cut into ¼-inch-thick wedges, and separated

3 large garlic cloves, minced

¼ cup Shrimp Paste Sauce (page 167)

1 tablespoon light brown sugar

1 tablespoon freshly ground black pepper

¼ cup chicken stock or water

1 tablespoon thinly sliced shallot

6 scallions, white and light-green parts cut into 1-inch pieces, dark green tops thinly sliced

1 lemongrass stalk, pale green and white parts only (see page 17)

6 Thai red chilies, smashed with the side of a large knife

2 makrut lime leaves, torn

2 tablespoons fresh lime juice

1 tablespoon fish sauce

### FOR SERVING

Thinly sliced shallot, for garnish

½ red long hot chili, sliced

Lime wedges, for squeezing

Jasmine Rice (page 234)

1  Marinate the pork: Place the sliced pork in a large airtight container. Add the oil, fish sauce, salt, sugar, baking soda, black pepper, and white pepper. Gently mix the marinade ingredients into the pork until everything is evenly distributed. Cover and marinate for 2 hours at room temperature or overnight in the refrigerator. (Remove the meat from the refrigerator 20 minutes before cooking.)

*recipe continues*

2   **Cook the stir-fry:** Set a wok over high heat and let it heat up until it begins to smoke. Add the vegetable oil and let it heat until it is restless in the pan and just begins to smoke. Immediately add the onion and garlic and stir-fry until the onion is translucent.

3   Add the pork to the hot wok and use two wooden or silicone spatulas to keep the pork moving in the pan, just like you would toss a big salad, continuously scooping along the bottom of the wok from the sides toward the middle. When the pork is about halfway cooked, add the shrimp paste sauce, brown sugar, black pepper, and chicken stock. Stir-fry with the two spatulas until everything is evenly distributed. Add the shallot, scallion whites, and the white parts of the lemongrass. Stir-fry with the spatulas just until combined, then add the smashed chilies, light green parts of the scallions, and the lime leaves, lime juice, and fish sauce.

4   Take the wok off the heat. Transfer the pork and sauce to a serving bowl.

5   **To serve:** Garnish with some sliced shallots, the reserved scallion tops, and sliced chili. Serve lime wedges for squeezing. Serve with cooked rice.

# kapi sauce (shrimp paste sauce)

**MAKES ABOUT 1 CUP**

3 medium garlic cloves, peeled but whole

1 medium shallot, sliced

10 Thai red chilies, stemmed but whole

3 tablespoons shrimp paste

4 tablespoons fish sauce

2 tablespoons light brown sugar

2 tablespoons fresh lime juice

½ to 1 teaspoon kosher salt

In a food processor, combine the garlic, shallot, and Thai chilies. Pulse until the vegetables are very finely chopped. Add the shrimp paste, fish sauce, 3 tablespoons water, and the brown sugar. Pulse until the mixture is smooth and uniform in color. Scrape the sauce into a medium bowl and stir in the lime juice and salt. Store in an airtight container in the refrigerator for weeks.

# POO PAD PONG KAREE
## stir-fried crab in curry powder sauce

Keep it moving! Your ingredients, that is! This amazing crab stir-fry comes together in less than 15 minutes. Because crab comes already cooked in the can, you're basically just stir-frying aromatics, whisking in eggs and milk, and then finishing it with crab.

Use a lot of crab, and if you are really feeling luxurious, use the best crab you can get—this dish deserves it, and you deserve it!

This dish is a showcase of how we incorporate the ingredients from Western and immigrant cuisines in new ways, making a creamy, fragrant crab "curry" that has amazing flavor but tastes so different from how Thai curries usually taste. This is an illustration of the many cultural influences in our cuisine: the Chinese would use evaporated milk, curry powder is inspired by Indian spice blends, and "long hots" (chilies) come from Central and South America. It's the whole world in your wok!

A wok is vital here because this recipe cooks very fast and you need a lot of surface to toss it. You will get that lovely flavor imparted by the breath of the wok. It cooks so quickly and delicately you don't have to chase your ingredients all over the pan.

1 tablespoon Nok's Karee Powder (page 56) or store-bought Madras curry powder

1 teaspoon paprika

1 tablespoon minced garlic

2 tablespoons Mom's Chili Jam (page 257, Nam Prik Phao)

½ cup thinly sliced yellow onion

1 bunch scallions, cut into 2-inch pieces (1 cup), plus more for garnish

2 stalks Chinese celery, ends trimmed, roughly chopped (see Note, page 154), plus more for garnish

2 red long hot chilies, thinly sliced on the diagonal

1 egg yolk

1 large egg

Freshly ground black pepper

Ground white pepper

¼ cup soy sauce

¼ cup packed light brown sugar

¼ cup plus 2 tablespoons canola or vegetable oil

1 cup canned crabmeat, jumbo or colossal if you want to be luxurious, plus a little more for garnish

6 tablespoons unsweetened evaporated milk

1  In a small bowl, mix together the karee powder, ½ teaspoon of the paprika, the minced garlic, and the chili jam.

2  In a medium bowl, combine the onion, scallions, Chinese celery, and chilies.

3  In a small bowl, combine the egg yolk and whole egg. Add a big pinch of black pepper, a big pinch of white pepper, the soy sauce, and brown sugar and whisk until smooth.

4  Set a large wok over high heat and let it heat up until it begins to smoke. Add ¼ cup of the oil and let it heat up until it is restless in the pan and just begins to smoke. Immediately add the garlic and spice mix and sauté until fragrant. Add the vegetables and stir-fry for a minute or two, until bright green and just barely tender. Add the egg mixture and cook for a minute, stirring constantly. Stir in the crabmeat and evaporated milk and turn off the heat.

5  In a small saucepan, combine the remaining ½ teaspoon paprika and 2 tablespoons oil. Heat over high heat just until fragrant, then pour the mixture over the stir-fry.

6  Garnish with more crabmeat, Chinese celery, and scallions.

**Serve with:** Jasmine Rice (page 234).

# GAI PAD KRATIEM

## garlic & black pepper chicken

Once you have the meat marinated, you can cook this faster than grabbing an Amazon package from your front stoop.

This dish is lean and light, with the chicken coated in a sauce of garlic, soy sauce, and lots of freshness from scallion and cilantro. While there is a good amount of oil, the fat is countered by the herbs; people in Thailand don't feel bloated after eating because we eat the right flavors together.

Make a batch of this on a lazy Sunday and portion it throughout the week if you are into that, or it's an easy breezy dinner. You can make this dish really quickly and add vegetables. Always serve it with rice.

Premince fresh garlic and make your life easy. Having minced garlic in your fridge is a game changer. Don't spend a lot of time chopping garlic before you cook.

**MARINATED CHICKEN**

¼ cup soy sauce

2 tablespoons canola oil

1 tablespoon sesame oil

1 tablespoon freshly ground black pepper

½ to 1 teaspoon kosher salt

1½ pounds chicken tenders, cut into long, thin strips

**STIR-FRY**

½ cup canola or vegetable oil

¾ cup roughly chopped garlic

¼ cup water

1 tablespoon Thai black soy sauce

1 tablespoon soy sauce

Kosher salt

1 cup thinly sliced scallions

¼ cup packed fresh cilantro leaves

1  **Marinate the chicken:** In a large bowl, whisk together the soy sauce, canola oil, sesame oil, pepper, and salt. Put the chicken strips in the bowl, and toss. Cover and refrigerate for 30 minutes or up to overnight.

2  **Make the stir-fry:** Set a large cast-iron skillet, wok, or Dutch oven over high heat. When the skillet starts to smoke, pour in the oil and let it heat up until you see wisps of smoke. Add the marinated chicken and garlic, and toss. Add the water, Thai soy sauce, regular soy sauce, and a big pinch of salt and stir-fry until the chicken is cooked through, about 5 minutes.

3  Take the skillet off the heat and stir in the scallions and cilantro leaves. Serve immediately with rice.

**Serve with:** Jasmine Rice (page 234).

# KANA PLA KEM
## chinese broccoli *with* salted fish

Salted fish is a staple food in most Southern Thai homes, and one piece of salted fish goes such a long way to feed a family. The flavor is funky and salty, powerful and delicious.

We mostly use it as a seasoning, in this case for a super quick stir-fry of Chinese broccoli. If you want to make this vegetarian, you can use Thai fermented bean paste or even miso instead; it won't taste the same at all, but will be delicious. The point is that you are using a salty, fermented ingredient for depth.

This recipe uses a technique my mother taught me when I was little, where the ingredients are cooked all together and quickly done because of the heat and the steam from the vegetables themselves.

Now smile, follow my recipe, and wait for the miracle to happen. When in doubt, don't trust yourself, trust me.

⅓ cup vegetable or canola oil

1 pound Chinese broccoli, chopped into 3-inch pieces

3 tablespoons minced garlic

5 Thai chilies, smashed

Big pinch of kosher salt

Pinch of freshly ground black pepper

Pinch of ground white pepper, plus more to finish

1 tablespoon sugar

1 tablespoon crumbled salted fish, Thai fermented soybean paste (tao jiew), or white miso

2 tablespoons soy sauce

1  Set a large wok over high heat and let it heat up until it begins to smoke. Add the oil and let it heat up until it is restless in the pan and just begins to smoke. Immediately add the Chinese broccoli, garlic, chilies, salt, black pepper, white pepper, sugar, and salted fish. Cook for 1 to 2 minutes without stirring (this will let the vegetables steam). Then toss and stir-fry until the broccoli is bright green and just tender, 1 to 2 minutes more. Add the soy sauce and stir-fry for another 30 seconds.

2  Transfer the stir-fry to a bowl or platter and sprinkle with a pinch of white pepper.

**Serve with:** Jasmine Rice (page 234).

# MOO WAAN
## my mother's caramelized pork

SERVES 4 TO 6

Do you like bacon? I'm about to show you a marriage of flavor that is even better than bacon.

Pork belly is cooked low and slow with shallots, palm sugar, fish sauce, and soy sauce until it's caramelized into a rich, beautiful, burnished orange. Have a sip of wine and enjoy the process. You will love this. Your babies will love this and Aunty Nok will be the favorite person in your house for sharing this recipe.

Moo waan can be a breakfast, a snack, or a dinner, and also can be a delicious one-plate meal with rice. Or do what I do with it: Serve it alongside spicy curries to balance them with its sweet richness.

And don't even think of throwing the fat away. You can use it in everything—from spreading it on bread to putting it in your tomato sauce.

¾ cup vegetable or canola oil

3 cups thinly sliced shallots

¼ cup roughly chopped garlic

1¾ pounds pork belly, cut into bite-size pieces

2 (70g) discs palm sugar or ½ cup brown sugar

2 tablespoons Thai black soy sauce

2 tablespoons fish sauce

Kosher salt

Freshly ground black pepper

Ground white pepper

1   In large cast-iron skillet, combine the oil, 2 cups of the shallots, and the garlic. Cook over high heat until the shallots are just turning translucent, 3 to 5 minutes.

2   Add the pork belly, reduce the heat to medium, and cook, stirring frequently, until the pork is no longer pink, about 10 minutes. Spread it in an even layer and reduce the heat to low. Cook until the fat is almost translucent and the meat is fork-tender and gives only a little resistance when you pierce it with a sharp paring knife, 20 to 25 minutes.

3   Add the palm sugar and cook, stirring, until the sugar is fully dissolved. Stir in the black soy sauce and fish sauce. Then stir in a big pinch each of salt, black pepper, and white pepper. Let the fat settle on top of the pork belly, and use a ladle to skim as much of it as you can into a heatproof container or jar (reserve the fat, and once it's cooled, seal and keep it in the fridge to spread on toast or use for cooking).

4   When you've removed as much fat as you can without taking out any of the dark sauce, turn the heat to high and add ¼ cup water. Cook, stirring, until all the pork pieces are coated in the thick, syrupy sauce. Then stir in the remaining shallots and turn off the heat.

**Serve with:** Jasmine Rice (page 234), and a spicy curry of your choice.

# NUA PAD LOOK PAK CHEE
## party-perfect coriander beef

This is a forgotten recipe. No one makes this anymore, so I'm bringing it back! It's a recipe that is originally from Indonesia. I remember this from my childhood, but couldn't find it when I was an adult, so I adapted this recipe to the flavors from my memory. It's simple, with a depth of flavor, a powerful aroma of floral coriander seeds, and a gentle heat from the pepper. It's so sweet and layered, like beef candy! It's a good accompaniment for spicy curry.

**MARINATED BEEF**

2 pounds boneless beef chuck roast (don't trim the fat; see Notes), cut into 2-inch slices

¼ cup fish sauce

1 tablespoon ground white pepper

2 tablespoons freshly ground black pepper

2 tablespoons light brown sugar

**FOR COOKING**

¾ cup vegetable or canola oil

½ cup roughly chopped garlic

3 (70g) discs palm sugar or ¾ cup light brown sugar

1 teaspoon to ½ tablespoon kosher salt

¼ cup tamarind concentrate (see page 22)

1 tablespoon fish sauce

½ cup coriander seeds, toasted and coarsely ground (see page 18)

1. **Marinate the beef:** Put the beef in an airtight container and sprinkle with the fish sauce, white pepper, black pepper, and brown sugar. Gently mix the seasonings into the meat until all the pieces are evenly coated. Then seal the container and refrigerate overnight.

2. **Cook the dish:** In a Dutch oven or cast-iron pot, combine the oil and garlic and cook over high heat, stirring frequently, just until the garlic is sizzling. Add the beef, stir to distribute the garlic, and use a wooden spoon to pat out the beef to cover the whole bottom of the pot. Cook without stirring for 2 minutes, stir, and cook for another 2 minutes, stirring frequently, until the meat is no longer pink.

3. Add ¼ cup water and reduce the heat to medium. Cook, uncovered, stirring every few minutes, until the beef is fork-tender or gives a little resistance when you pierce it with a sharp paring knife, 10 to 15 minutes.

4. Add the palm sugar and cook, stirring (breaking up the palm sugar, if that's what you're using), until the sugar is fully dissolved, 5 to 7 minutes.

5. Increase the heat to high. Add the salt and tamarind concentrate and cook, stirring, until the oil separates on top and the sauce coats the beef, about 5 minutes, depending on the size of your pot. Stir in the fish sauce and coriander. Cook for another minute or two to glaze the beef, then turn off the heat.

6. Tilt the pot so all the oil pools on one side, then use a spoon or ladle to scoop out the clear fat into a heatproof container or jar (see Notes). Transfer the beef and dark-colored sauce to a plate or bowl.

**Serve with:** Sticky Rice (page 236) and any spicy curry.

**NOTES**
- Don't trim the fat off the beef, or I will be very upset. The fat makes the meat tender.
- Please don't add the palm sugar too early or the beef will take forever to cook. We need to get things beautiful and bubbling!
- Save the oil from cooking the beef because it's perfect for making fried rice. Once it's cooled, seal and keep it in the fridge.

# GOONG PAD NAM PRIK PHAO

## shrimp & chili jam stir-fry

**SERVES 4**

We always got fresh seafood when the fishermen arrived in the morning at the market. So much of our cooking centered around what was available that day. One thing we would often do with shrimp is simply stir-fry it with nam prik phao—you have it made and are keeping it in the fridge like I told you to, right?—soy sauce, onions, and garlic. Serve it with rice and dinner is ready in 10 minutes.

When you eat it, don't spare your compliments. I'm ready for them.

### SAUCE

¼ cup Mom's Chili Jam (page 257, Nam Prik Pao), or chili paste in soybean oil from a Chinese grocery store

1 tablespoon soy sauce

Big pinch of freshly ground black pepper

Big pinch of ground white pepper

1 tablespoon light brown sugar

### STIR-FRY

¼ cup canola or vegetable oil

1 medium white or yellow onion, quartered and sliced ¼ inch thick, pieces separated (2 cups)

5 large garlic cloves, roughly chopped

1 pound jumbo shrimp (see Note), peeled and deveined

1 bunch scallions, cut into 2-inch pieces (1 packed cup)

2 red long hot chilies, thinly sliced on the diagonal

1  **Make the sauce:** In a small bowl, whisk together the chili jam, ¼ cup water, soy sauce, black pepper, white pepper, and brown sugar until smooth. Set aside.

2  **Make the stir-fry:** Set a wok or large cast-iron skillet over high heat and let it heat up until it begins to smoke. Add the oil and let it heat up until it is restless in the pan and just begins to smoke. Immediately add the onion and stir-fry until translucent, 3 to 5 minutes. Add the garlic and stir-fry for 15 to 20 seconds. Pour in the sauce and stir everything together. Add the shrimp and stir again until all the shrimp are coated. Spread out the shrimp in a single layer, leave the pan alone, and meditate for a minute or two, until the shrimp are just opaque.

3  Toss in the scallions and chilies and stir-fry just until the scallions are bright green and start to soften.

**Serve with:** Jasmine Rice (page 234).

NOTE: I like jumbo shrimp for this because there is less chance of overcooking them, but use what you like. Save the shells and freeze them until you have enough to make Shrimp Shell Stock (page 146). You can use frozen deveined shrimp here; just be sure to thaw them before you cook them.

# PAD MA KUA YAOW
## my mother's colorful stir-fried eggplant

This was my mom's recipe. She doesn't cook much anymore, so I want to share her recipes with the world so I will always remember her food.

The green, red, and purple colors of this dish are gorgeous. The purple of the eggplant is bright and shiny, like an amethyst, and there is so much basil, it's used more like a green vegetable than just an herb for a little aroma. Don't worry about the oil initially; it's supposed to be a little greasy; you will balance the fat with rice, because the flavors of the bean paste sauce will make you want to eat more rice. The dish is sweet, with the gentlest hit of heat. It's the perfect vegan recipe.

Just remember to keep it all moving in the pan just until the basil is wilted. Otherwise the ingredients will get oxidized, and we don't like oxidation because it turns everything a murky brown. You want beauty, you want a rainbow!

**SAUCE**

3 tablespoons Thai fermented soybean paste (tao jiew) or white miso

1 tablespoon light brown sugar

1 tablespoon sesame oil

1 tablespoon soy sauce

Big pinch of kosher salt

Pinch of freshly ground black pepper

Pinch of ground white pepper

**STIR-FRY**

¼ cup canola or vegetable oil

2 Chinese eggplants, cut into 1-inch pieces or thin rounds

5 large garlic cloves, finely chopped

2 cups packed fresh Thai basil leaves

2 red long hot chilies, thinly sliced on the diagonal

1   **Make the sauce:** In a small bowl, whisk together the soybean paste, brown sugar, 2 tablespoons water, the sesame oil, soy sauce, salt, black pepper, and white pepper until smooth. Set aside.

2   **Make the stir-fry:** Set a wok or large cast-iron skillet over high heat and let it heat up until it begins to smoke. Add the oil and let it heat up until it is restless in the pan and just begins to smoke. Immediately add the eggplant and stir-fry until it is soft and just beginning to brown, 1 to 3 minutes.

3   Stir in the reserved sauce, the garlic, basil, and chilies, and stir-fry just until the basil is wilted, 1 to 2 minutes.

**Serve with:** Jasmine Rice (page 234).

# PAD PAK KAD DONG
## comforting pickled mustard greens *with* eggs

This is a simple dish that uses store-bought pickled mustard greens, which are a little like if you imagine a nonspicy, sweet/sour/salty kimchi. It has a lot of flavor and umami, and is delicious balanced with rice. We soak the greens in water for an hour (or boil them for a few minutes if you don't have time) to take out some of the salt and mellow it out, then stir-fry with soy sauce, garlic, and eggs. It's another dish that's a great accompaniment on the table next to spicy foods.

This is Southern Thai comfort food that is easy and happy. No one at the table will be able to stop eating it.

**SAUCE**

2 tablespoons soy sauce

2 tablespoons light brown sugar

Big pinch of kosher salt

Pinch of freshly ground black pepper

Pinch of ground white pepper

**STIR-FRY**

3 tablespoons canola or vegetable oil

3 large eggs

Pinch of kosher salt

Pinch of freshly ground black pepper

Pinch of ground white pepper

5 large garlic cloves, roughly chopped

1 cup (packed) pickled mustard greens cut into 1-inch strips (see Note)

1 red long hot chili, thinly sliced on the diagonal

1 tablespoon thinly sliced scallion

1  Make the sauce: In a small bowl, whisk together the soy sauce, brown sugar, salt, black pepper, and white pepper until smooth. Set aside.

2  Make the stir-fry: Set a wok or large cast-iron skillet over high heat and let it heat up until it begins to smoke. Add the oil, then add the eggs, salt, black pepper, white pepper, garlic, pickled mustard greens, and the reserved sauce. Stir-fry, scrambling the eggs, until the eggs are soft and scrambled.

3  Remove from the heat, stir in the chilies and scallion, and serve.

**Serve with:** Jasmine Rice (page 234).

NOTE: Soak the pickled mustard greens for 1 hour in cold water to cover, or boil them for 3 minutes before using.

*183*

# TAO HU PAD HOR RA PA HED
## basil tofu & mushroom

This is an excellent recipe for vegetarians because it is hearty and simple and uses pantry ingredients that you probably always have on hand. The mushrooms have a meaty quality, the tofu has a crisp skin and soft bite, and the basil rounds out the dish.

Button mushrooms are often used for Chinese New Year or weddings. In Thailand, we often use canned mushrooms, but here you can use fresh ones. The basil is used as a green here and adds an earthy brightness to the dish. I don't care what basil you use, just don't use kale.

Have you looked online for fried tofu recipes? There are a hundred ways to do it. There is no need to be a rocket scientist about frying tofu. Just pat it dry before you fry it and make sure you wait until it turns golden. If you can get store-bought fried tofu, you can use that. To save time, mince the garlic and chili together in a mini food processor or mash them together in a mortar and pestle.

### SAUCE

2 tablespoons soy sauce

1 tablespoon light brown sugar

Big pinch of kosher salt

Pinch of freshly ground black pepper

Pinch of ground white pepper

### STIR-FRY

1 (14-ounce) package extra-firm tofu

¼ cup vegetable oil (or enough to coat the bottom of the pan)

8 ounces white (button) mushrooms, stemmed and quartered

5 large garlic cloves, chopped

1 red long hot chili or 3 Thai chilies, finely chopped

2 cups packed fresh basil leaves

1  **Make the sauce:** In a small bowl, whisk together the soy sauce, 2 tablespoons water, the brown sugar, salt, black pepper, and white pepper until smooth. Set aside.

2  **Make the stir-fry:** Pat the tofu block dry with paper towels and then cut it into 1-inch cubes. Blot them with paper towels to absorb as much moisture as possible.

3  Line a plate with paper towels and have it within arm's length of the stove. Set a wok or large cast-iron skillet over high heat and let it heat up until it begins to smoke. Add the oil and let it heat up until it is restless in the pan and just begins to smoke. Immediately add the tofu and cook, using two wooden spatulas to turn it, until the pieces are browned on all sides, about 1 minute. Transfer the fried tofu to the paper towels to drain, leaving the oil in the skillet.

4  Put the wok or skillet back over high heat, add the mushrooms, and stir-fry until they start to soften, about 2 minutes. Return the tofu to the pan, along with the garlic and chilies, and stir-fry for 30 seconds until it's evenly combined.

5  Pour the reserved sauce around the edges of the pan and stir-fry to coat everything in the sauce. Add the basil and stir-fry just until the basil is wilted.

**Serve with:** Jasmine Rice (page 234).

# KALUM THOD NAM PLA
## the most outstanding three-ingredient cabbage

SERVES 4

This dish is so simple, just seared/charred cabbage with a sweet-salty fish and palm sugar sauce. In the restaurant, when people complain a curry is too spicy or salty, I send out this cabbage dish to balance the heat, and it makes everyone smile.

For some people cabbage is a comfort food and some people see it as a difficult food, but for me cabbage is my home and the food I grew up with. My mom always made this dish for me when I came home from college.

This takes 2 minutes to make, but if you don't want to stir-fry, or if you are already out in the backyard, you can grill this cabbage and pour the sauce over.

The key here is to char the cabbage; this keeps it crispy and gives it a good smoky flavor. So make sure that the cabbage is well charred.

You will be surprised at how a simple cabbage dish will be the one everyone remembers for a long time.

2 (70g) discs palm sugar or ½ cup brown sugar

3 tablespoons fish sauce

⅓ cup canola or vegetable oil

1 pound flat Korean cabbage, leaves separated, stacked, and roughly cut into 2-inch pieces,

1 In a small skillet or saucepan, combine the palm sugar, fish sauce, and 2 tablespoons water and cook over low heat, stirring frequently and breaking up the palm sugar with a wooden spoon, until the sugar is fully melted and the mixture looks smooth (the time will vary depending on the form of palm sugar you have). Remove the skillet from the heat and set it aside.

2 Set a wok or large cast-iron skillet over high heat and let it heat up until it begins to smoke. Add the oil and let it heat up until it is restless in the pan and just begins to smoke. Add the cabbage and don't do anything for 1 minute. Grab two wooden spatulas and flip the cabbage and spread it out in the pan. Don't you dare cover that pan; when there's steam, there's no char. After another minute, stir it again and repeat one more time, until about half of the cabbage pieces have char marks.

3 Pour the sauce around the sides of the pan and stir-fry with the two spatulas, flipping the cabbage until everything is coated. Continue stir-frying until the thickest pieces of cabbage are tender, making sure to keep things moving in the wok so the sauce doesn't burn. Transfer to a bowl or plate. Serve with any of your favorite recipes and make your soul happy.

# STIR-FRIES ARE FOR BUSY PEOPLE

It's Monday morning, and Titi is eating my Prada shoes. Part-time Pomeranian and full-time paper shredder (with very fine tastes), he is my beloved companion and confidant, and we are about to start our day together. I clean up the designer mess and head down to my kitchen to have an iced coffee and a pastry, then start reading the day's report for my restaurant, Kalaya. I call my husband to share a moment of connection while he is traveling abroad, and then slip into my Gucci furry loafers and head out the door.

When I get to the restaurant, the block smells like soup stock, cinnamon, and cloves, and never has any street corner smelled so good. There is a sour curry known as Caeng Som Pak Thai (page 118) boiling away in a giant pot, and it feels like home. I check on my team and can hear one of the chefs butchering the meat wrong; the knife has no rhythm through the meat, the symphony of the kitchen is interrupted. I run over to show him the way that preserves the integrity of the meat. I take a few calls, have a meeting with my partners, and stop to stir the giant pot of sour curry. It is like magic.

I look at my 140-seat restaurant, checking out the way the light shines in through the skylight and the cathedral windows. I admire the giant trees from my hometown in the center. I've come a long way in this city, but I was destined for this life. From pushing my mom's curry paste cart, to working with customers at her stall and later learning about hospitality as a flight attendant, I am sure everything in my life has led to this. I remember how my mother always said, be generous, good, and gracious, and good things will happen.

We get ready for our staff lunch; it's meatball subs today. Some days the team cooks Italian, and other days Mediterranean, but whatever they cook, they cook with intuition and heart, and there is beauty when everyone eats together and chats about their life as we get ready for dinner service.

Tonight, there will be families, first dates, graduations, and retirements coming through here. There will be people who have never tried a curry in their life, and people who have visited Thailand, and people who come here because it's on all the restaurant hot lists. There will be loyal veteran customers, colleagues, and new folks who may become loyal customers one day. I visit each table, touch each table, talk to each customer, to make sure that everyone who walks through my restaurant is feeling happy and satisfied. I will help the people eating curry all by itself and send out other dishes to help balance the flavor, I will carry babies around the restaurant, go back to the kitchen and check on my staff, and meet the next seating until closing. And tomorrow I will do it all again.

I'm like Mom in this way. She was always working, always busy. She worked every day of the year; her only day off was Chinese New Year. All day, every day, she would work hard at her curry stall in the market and then come home to take care of us.

Like so many women everywhere who are balancing work and taking care of family, she didn't have a lot of time to talk when she got home. After work, her next focus was to make sure everyone was fed. She would rush into the kitchen, and we would watch her cook and help where we could. Watching her make a Southern Thai stir-fry like Pad Ma Kua Yaow (a beautiful stir-fried eggplant with basil and savory soy paste, page 180) or Moo Waan (a quick-caramelized pork belly, page 175) was magic. Her kitchen was the ultimate classroom for me, and those times I spent watching my mom as she cooked are my most cherished memories.

Just as she would get up early every day and never stop working to make sure her customers were satisfied and happy, I am determined to do the same.

# NUA THOD

## my mother's stir-fry beef

SERVES 4 TO 6

My mom never taught me how to cook outright. Instead I learned by observation, and through experience. No matter how hard her day was at the market, she would come home and cook and I would watch her. When we sat together at the table, it was the best time of day. To make this dish, nua thod, she would marinate beef overnight in sugar and fish sauce, and the next day there was a beautiful brown color and the meat fried so beautifully in its own fat to bring out the flavor. This recipe is beloved among many generations in my family. My dad loved it; my mother would make it for him, and now my nieces and nephews love it, too. We continue sharing the love through our food. This recipe reminds me of my mom's love and devotion to her family.

One night I came home and I had leftover beef, so I decided to boil the heck out of it with the seasonings until the water evaporated and it was soft. This was my shortcut, there was no marination, and it saved me time for my busy life in Philly. My mom cooked with better cuts of meat, but I adapted this recipe to what I had here and it came out good.

1 pound boneless beef
    chuck roast

3 tablespoons fish sauce

Big pinch of kosher salt

1 teaspoon ground
    white pepper

2 tablespoons light
    brown sugar

½ cup canola or
    vegetable oil

7 Thai chilies

5 makrut lime leaves

1   Cut the beef lengthwise into long strips ½ inch thick. Then cut each strip into 2-inch-long pieces.

2   Put the beef in a bowl and add the fish sauce, salt, white pepper, and brown sugar. Mix well with your hands, then scrape the seasoned meat into a medium saucepan or high-sided skillet (preferably nonstick) and add ½ cup water and the oil.

3   Put the pan over high heat, and when the liquid starts to boil, reduce the heat to medium and let the meat simmer and then eventually fry, stirring occasionally, until it is browned and beginning to caramelize, 15 to 20 minutes.

4   Increase the heat to high and cook, stirring frequently, until the meat is evenly caramelized on all sides, 2 to 5 minutes.

5   Add the chilies and lime leaves, stir until fragrant, and use a slotted spoon to transfer the meat to a serving bowl.

**Serve with:** Sticky Rice (page 236) and cucumber slices.

# MIENG PLA THOD
## fried branzino *with* herbs

SERVES 2 TO 4

This is dinner-party food, or you can make it for yourself because you deserve it. (Also turn on the stove exhaust or open the windows, because you deserve fresh air, too.) When you are done, the fried fish with a hill of raw fresh garnishes is waiting to be shared.

*Mieng* means "wrapped snack" or anything you eat in a leaf, so you eat this by putting bites of fish and garnishes in a leaf of lettuce and eating little wraps. The garnishes are intense—little bits of raw ginger, garlic, shallot, chilies, and lime—yes, you mince a whole lime, skin and all, because the tartness and bitterness balance everything and the effect is amazing. Every bite is so fresh and textural and bright! You will have sauce dripping down your hands and you will laugh and have a sip of beer and all will be good. You will say OMG, but it's not God, it's me!

**SAUCE**

10 Thai chilies

2 large garlic cloves

3 tablespoons light brown sugar

2 tablespoons fish sauce

6 tablespoons lime juice

½ to 1 teaspoon kosher salt

**FISH**

1 whole branzino (about 1 pound), cleaned

Kosher salt

Ground white pepper

Canola oil, for frying

¼ cup cashews

**FOR SERVING**

Butter lettuce leaves

3 large garlic cloves, thinly sliced

2 tablespoons minced, peeled ginger

1 large shallot, thinly sliced

1 tablespoon tiny cubes of lime, with the peel

1 red long hot chili, very thinly sliced

2 tablespoons chopped fresh cilantro

1 tablespoon Ground Dried Shrimp (page 137)

1  **Make the sauce:** With a mortar and pestle or in a food processor, grind together the chilies and garlic until very finely chopped. Add the brown sugar, fish sauce, lime juice, and salt and grind or process until everything is evenly combined. Pour the sauce into a small bowl.

2  **For the fish:** To butterfly the fish, use a sharp knife and kitchen shears to cut almost all the way through the belly of the fish, then open it up and use the shears to cut out the spine. If you have time, pull out any small bones you see. Rinse the fish under cool running water and pat it dry. (If possible, let it dry at room temperature, skin-side up, for about 30 minutes. This will help the skin get extra crispy when you fry the fish.) Season both sides of the fish with big pinches of salt and white pepper.

3  Set a wire rack over a baking sheet and line a plate with paper towels. Have both within arm's reach of the stove. Pour ½ inch of oil into a Dutch oven or other wide pot and put it over high heat. When the oil is smoking, carefully lay the fish in the pot, skin-side down. Fry for 2 to 3 minutes, pressing the fish flat with a spatula, until the skin is evenly golden brown. Then flip the fish and fry it on the other side until golden, until the flesh just begins to flake easily, another 1 or 2 minutes. Using two spatulas, carefully transfer the fish to the wire rack.

4  Add the cashews to the hot oil and fry over high heat until they are evenly browned, maybe 30 seconds. Transfer to the paper towels to drain.

5  **To serve:** Place the fish on an oval platter. Tuck the lettuce leaves under the fish (you will use these as wraps to eat the fish), then top with the fried cashews, sliced garlic, ginger, shallot, chopped lime, red chili, and cilantro. Sprinkle the ground dried shrimp over top.

6  To eat, fill lettuce leaves with pieces of fish (be careful of any lingering bones), scooping in some of the toppings; drizzle with the sauce and fold into little wraps.

# TAO HU TOD
## fried tofu

Okay, team, let's try not to think too hard with this one. It's tofu, fried until crispy and crunchy, then served with sweet chili sauce and peanuts; you are going to love it.

I know there are many tips out there about boiling the tofu, air-drying it, flouring and coating, whatever. Stop overanalyzing, you aren't getting a PhD in frying tofu. Relax. You just need to buy extra-firm tofu, and then pat, pat, pat it dry. The tofu will bubble in oil and get a beautiful golden crust.

If the tofu pieces stick together in the pan, don't try to separate them. They will separate when they fully cook.

1 (14-ounce) package extra-firm tofu, drained

Canola or vegetable oil, for frying

Sweet Chili Sauce (page 41, Nam Jim Waan)

Crushed peanuts, for garnish

1   Cut the block of tofu crosswise into 8 equal slices and then cut each piece diagonally to make 16 triangles. Pat the pieces very dry with paper towels and set aside. Making sure the tofu is dry will not only help with the crispiness, it will prevent hot oil from splattering when you add it to the pan.

2   Line a plate with paper towels and place it within arm's length of the stove. Pour ½ inch oil into a large deep skillet and set it over high heat. When the oil just starts to smoke, carefully add the tofu (lower it in with a strainer or tongs, or gently release it into the oil; don't just drop it in or it will splash on you, burn your hand, and ruin your beautiful clothes). Reduce the heat to medium and fry, turning the pieces occasionally, until deep golden brown, 10 to 13 minutes. If they stick together, don't worry; you can separate them after they're done cooking. Transfer the tofu to the paper towels to drain.

3   Serve at room temperature (we do not want people biting into hot tofu because there will be a lawsuit) with the sweet chili sauce and crushed peanuts.

# CAI THOD HAT YAI
## hat yai fried chicken

**SERVES 4 TO 6**

Forget KFC. This is the beloved Southern Thai fried chicken, specifically from the Southern city of Hat Yai. It showcases all of the classic Southern Thai ingredients; black pepper, white pepper, garlic, cilantro, and coriander, and you will enjoy it. Everyone in your family will love this chicken. Serve it with sticky rice for an easy weeknight meal. The skin will be so crispy and delicious, and the meat will be moist on the inside. Do not forget to pair this with dipping sauces, especially Nam Jim Waan (page 41, Sweet Chili Sauce). The sweet heat from the dipping sauce brings out the best in the texture and flavor of the chicken.

If you are really tired, you could experiment with this in the air fryer and it won't be as crispy, but what matters is you tried.

¼ cup fish sauce

5 garlic cloves, roughly chopped

¼ cup chopped cilantro stems

1 tablespoon light brown sugar

4 large boneless (see Note), skin-on chicken thighs (about 1½ pounds total)

1½ tablespoons freshly ground black pepper

1½ tablespoons ground white pepper

2 tablespoons ground coriander

4 drops orange food coloring

¼ cup rice flour

Canola or vegetable oil, for shallow-frying

### FOR SERVING
Sticky Rice (page 236)

Sweet Chili Sauce (page 41, Nam Jim Waan)

Fried Shallots (page 45)

1   With a mortar and pestle or in a food processor, grind together the fish sauce, garlic, cilantro stems, and brown sugar until smooth.

2   Score the flesh side of the chicken with a sharp knife. Put the chicken in a large bowl, and add the fish sauce/cilantro mixture, the black pepper, white pepper, coriander, food coloring, and rice flour. Mix well, massaging the seasonings into the chicken. Cover and refrigerate for 30 minutes.

3   Line a plate with paper towels and place it within arm's length of the stove. Pour ½ inch oil into a wide deep skillet or Dutch oven (preferably nonstick) and put it over high heat. When the oil starts to smoke, reduce the heat to medium and add the chicken, skin-side down. Fry until browned and crispy on one side, about 5 minutes, then flip the chicken. Fry, pressing down on the chicken with a spatula, until the chicken is fully cooked, another 5 minutes. Transfer to the paper towels.

4   **To serve:** Serve with rice, sweet chili sauce as a dipping sauce, and fried shallots.

NOTE: If you can find only bone-in, skin-on chicken thighs, use kitchen shears to cut out the bones yourself, but keep the skin on.

# YAANG

200

**In the United States, the grill is usually thought of as a man's world; men and their meat get praise for what usually is a simple process.**

People are always surprised that I am a master at the grill, and yet this is the way we grew up. We learned how to grill from an early age. The marinades and accompanying dips were a way to showcase your signature family recipes.

We use charcoal, but that smoky char can be achieved even on an electric grill. The range of what we grill is far beyond steak—we grill everything from rice to organ meat to fruits like pineapple and watermelon, where the natural sugars make it like candy.

The North of Thailand is known for their grilled herb sausages, and Issan, the Northeast, is known for their grilled chicken and sticky rice, but in the South, we are known for our use of coconut milk in the marinade, which adds a delicate sweetness to grilled recipes, and our love of grilling seafood. Grilling allows a beautiful color; the marinade and the meats fuse together and really shine. The recipes in this chapter—like Gai Yaang Kamin (page 204, Grilled Turmeric Chicken with Sweet Chili Sauce) or a very quick Nua Yaang (page 203, Grilled Beef with Thai Chili Dipping Sauce)—draw from all over Thailand, but carry my family's Southern accent.

These are meals where you invite your friends over on a summer afternoon and eat with your hands, or off skewers. You can pair these recipes with sticky rice and other salads and sides for a very easy and relaxed meal. They may be a little more involved than just throwing on a hamburger or hot dog, but they're so much more delicious than that.

And for the women who take the helm of the grill for these recipes, enjoy your success and accept the compliments with pride. Don't be humble, you have earned this.

YAANG

# NUA YAANG

## grilled beef *with* thai chili dipping sauce

**SERVES 4**

Whenever my mom found a good cut of steak, she would make this. While nua yaang is found throughout Thailand, this is a family recipe that sets itself apart with black and white pepper. This simple and elegant steak is salty and umami-rich, and the pairing with Seafood Sauce (page 34, Nam Jim Seafood) or Charred Aromatic Tamarind Chili Dipping Sauce (page 38, Nam Jim Jaew) is beautiful and balanced. What makes a simple marinated protein shine is the different sauces you can pair it with and the sticky rice to go with it.

This steak comes together super fast; massaging the powerful marinade into the meat allows you to get away with a very fast marinating time—no more than 30 minutes is needed, and you could even just rub on the seasonings and cook right away.

1 pound skirt steak

1 tablespoon finely chopped garlic

2 tablespoons fish sauce

½ to 1 teaspoon kosher salt

½ teaspoon freshly ground black pepper

½ teaspoon ground white pepper

2 tablespoons chopped fresh cilantro

1 tablespoon canola oil

**FOR SERVING**

Seafood Sauce (page 34, Nam Jim Seafood)

Charred Aromatic Tamarind Chili Dipping Sauce (page 38, Nam Jim Jaew)

Chopped fresh cilantro

Sliced red chilies

Sliced scallions

Sticky Rice (page 236)

1   Poke the beef all over on both sides with a fork.

2   Put the beef in a large bowl. Add the garlic, fish sauce, salt, black pepper, white pepper, cilantro, and oil. Gently mix with your hands until the beef is evenly covered with the seasonings. If you have time, let it sit for 30 minutes, otherwise move to the next step.

3   Set your grill to medium-high heat. Clean and oil the grates.

4   Add the steak to the grates and grill until medium-rare inside and nicely charred outside, for 2 to 3 minutes per side. Let the steak rest for 2 minutes after cooking.

5   Slice across the grain with the knife at an angle, add to the cutting board, and serve with the sauces, cilantro, chilies, scallion, and sticky rice.

# GAI YAANG KAMIN
## grilled turmeric chicken *with* sweet chili sauce

**SERVES 4**

Ko Tah was a vendor in our village who sold this dish. He had a coffee shop and his gai yaang was so amazing. He's not there anymore, but when I walk by where his stall used to be, I travel back in time. He made it with his own oil barrel cut in half as the grill, and yet his gai yaang was so luxurious. When my father had money from a paycheck or gambling winnings, he would go and buy this gai yaang for us. It's very special and it's the smell that sticks in my mind. When you are young and poor, everything is so intriguing. I used to say that one day when I have money, I will go and buy grilled stingray (because it made me feel all the umami) and this grilled chicken. Now I make this gai yaang from my memory. It's luxurious because of the melding of the coconut cream and the sweetness of the fish sauce in the glaze. And in the South, we use turmeric, and more warm spices, which sets this apart.

I love to share this with my family, friends, and customers. There is something that is satisfying when you can make your childhood wish a reality.

This recipe is written for half a chicken, to be part of a larger meal with other dishes, but feel free to double the recipe to use the whole chicken.

**MARINATED CHICKEN**

1 tablespoon fish sauce

1 teaspoon Thai black soy sauce

1 tablespoon ground turmeric

½ teaspoon kosher salt

½ teaspoon freshly ground black pepper

½ teaspoon ground white pepper

½ chicken (in one piece), including the wing, breast, thigh, and drumstick

**GLAZE**

½ cup coconut cream (see Note)

1 tablespoon fish sauce

1 tablespoon light brown sugar

½ tablespoon minced garlic

½ tablespoon Nok's Karee Powder (page 56) or store-bought organic Madras curry powder

¼ teaspoon freshly ground black pepper

¼ teaspoon ground white pepper

1  **Marinate the chicken:** In a bowl large enough to hold the half chicken, combine the fish sauce, black soy sauce, turmeric, salt, black pepper, and white pepper. Add the chicken and rub the marinade over. Cover and refrigerate overnight.

2  **Make the glaze:** In a skillet, stir together the coconut cream, fish sauce, brown sugar, garlic, karee powder, black pepper, and white pepper. Set over high heat and as soon as it starts to bubble, remove from the heat and set aside.

3  Preheat a grill to medium-high heat. Clean and oil the grates. Set the chicken on the grates skin-side down. Grill until the skin is golden brown but not yet blackened, 10 to 12 minutes. Flip the chicken and grill until the thickest parts register 165°F on an instant-read thermometer, about another 10 minutes. (The cooking time will vary, depending on the temperature of your grill.)

4  Cut the grilled chicken into pieces and put them in a large bowl. Pour in the glaze and turn to coat.

**Serve with:** Some chopped cilantro and Sweet Chili Sauce (page 41) for dipping. Eat this with your hands and Sticky Rice (page 256). Live luxuriously.

NOTE: If your coconut cream is very solid, pop it into a microwave-safe bowl and microwave for 30 seconds. If you don't have coconut cream but have coconut milk, reduce the coconut milk by half in a saucepan.

# COONG PHAO AND PLA MUEK YAANG
## grilled prawns & three-minute grilled squid

It's time to build your Southern Thai grilled seafood platter. You can present these simply grilled prawns and squid as a centerpiece with dipping sauces, such as Nam Jim Seafood (page 34, Seafood Sauce) and Nam Jim Tao Jiew (page 33, Fermented Bean Sauce). Place crunchy palate cleansers such as cucumber, watermelon, and chopped long beans on the side to have fresh bites in between.

River prawns are my favorite thing to eat. The texture is fresh and fatty. They are grand in their presentation and are raised in freshwater. These grilled prawns will wow your guests, and the price is often better than lobster, and it's fresher and sweeter. These are beautiful and usually from Sri Lanka or Bangladesh. If you can't find river prawns, then you can use lobster.

If you are most used to seeing your squid fried in batter, this is clean, beautiful, and, in my opinion, the way squid should be enjoyed. The soda water makes the meat tighter and cleaner. The soy sauce/curry powder marinade makes the squid's flavor sweet and creamy, and the texture is never rubbery if you cook it fast and pay attention.

2 river prawns, thawed if frozen, feelers and legs trimmed off (about 1 pound each), or 2 small lobsters

1 pound cleaned skin-on fresh squid (see Note)

1 (12-ounce) can seltzer

2 tablespoons canola oil

Kosher salt and freshly ground black pepper

½ teaspoon ground white pepper

2 tablespoons Thai black soy sauce

1 tablespoon Nok's Karee Powder (page 56) or store-bought Madras curry powder

1 Preheat a grill to high heat. Clean and oil the grates.

2 Butterfly the river prawns using kitchen shears, cutting along the underside almost all the way through from the head to the tail, then opening them up like a book. Clean out the eggs and other innards under running water, and pat dry. If you're using lobsters, simply split them in half lengthwise. Don't worry about cleaning them.

3 Cut two crosswise slits through one side of each squid. (Meaning, don't cut all the way through the squid, just one side.) Put the squid in a large shallow bowl or baking dish and pour the seltzer over top. Let sit for 5 minutes. (This will make them very clean and improve the texture of the meat when it is grilled.)

4 Drain the squid and pat dry. In a medium bowl, toss the squid with the canola oil, a big pinch of salt, ½ teaspoon black pepper, the white pepper, black soy sauce, and karee powder. Stuff the tentacles of the squid into the bodies so they are easier to turn on the grill.

5 Season the flesh side of the prawns or lobster with salt and pepper.

6 Set the squid on the grill and cook until charred and just opaque, about 1½ minutes per side. Take the squid off the grill and cover with foil to keep warm.

7 Set the prawns on the grill, shell-side down, cover, and grill just until the flesh is opaque, 7 to 10 minutes. No flipping! If you flip it, the juices will spill and drip. When the prawns or lobster are just cooked through, carefully put them on a platter, holding them steady so the juices don't drop out. Don't doubt yourself, you can do this.

NOTE: Ask your fishmonger to clean the squid. They should take out the quill, the beak, and the guts.

# PLA PHAO
## grilled whole black bass

SERVES 4 TO 6

For some reason, I find that some Americans are still afraid of whole fish, and maybe it's growing up with fish sticks or only fillets, feeling disconnected and not being able to see where your food comes from. Be brave and embrace cooking a whole fish. When you serve it, the presentation is beautiful and everyone can dig into the part they like the most (fish cheek, anyone?), and when you grill the whole fish, you use the five senses to understand. You will hear the sizzle of the skin, which tells you it is crisping up and getting ready to release from the grill without ripping, you will smell the aromatics of gently smoking fish, and your neighbors will come and knock on your door because they are hungry.

Grill any whole fish you can get your hands on for an easy and delicious meal. Salt and oil on both sides, and grill it. Skin on, scales on. In Thailand, we eat the scales, but you can scrape them off or remove the skin to eat the fillet. Whole fish is so delicious, if you don't want to clean it, you don't have too. (Well, you can ask the fishmonger to gut it.)

When the fish is fresh, there is nothing else you need. Highlight the beauty of our ingredients.

1 whole black bass (1 to 2 pounds), scaled, gutted

1 tablespoon canola or vegetable oil

3 to 4 tablespoons kosher salt (depending on the size of your fish)

1. Preheat a grill to high heat. Clean and oil the grates. If your fish is thick, cut a couple of slashes through the flesh to let the heat penetrate.

2. Drizzle both sides of the fish with the oil, then sprinkle all over with the salt, pressing it into the fish.

3. Grill the fish on one side until it no longer sticks to the grates, about 8 minutes. Slide a fish spatula underneath it to release it. Then roll the fish over to flip it, and grill until the skin releases easily again and a paring knife slides in and out easily in the thick flesh just behind the head, about another 8 minutes.

4. Remove the fish from the grill, scrape off any visible salt, put it on a platter or cutting board, and let people pull out their own bones at the table.

**Serve with:** You can serve with seasonal vegetables, or make grilled black bass lettuce wraps. You can also serve this with rice and dipping sauces like Nam Jim Seafood (page 34, Seafood Sauce), or plate it with thinly sliced watermelon radishes for crunch and color.

# NUENG, OB & TOON

**Traditionally, we don't have ovens in most homes in Thailand. Many of us have outdoor kitchens, and this allows us to cook without heating up the house.**

Our kitchens might look different from those in North America; sometimes it's a burner hooked up to gas tank and a clay pot that also has room for hot charcoal.

In Thai kitchens, we "bake" on our stovetop, in clay pots, and our techniques can achieve the same kind of baked and braised qualities you get out of your oven for savory dishes. And we rely much more on methods like steaming for pure flavor and tender textures.

These recipes are meant to be quick and made in one pot so you have easy cleanup and peace of mind. When you steam a fish or meat, you are preserving so many essential nutrients and developing a soft and fluffy texture. These recipes will help you on a weeknight after work or for a weekend lunch with friends, but most of all they will show you how we innovate in Southern Thailand to bring out a diversity of flavors and textures in our food.

# PLA NUNG SEE EEW

## quick steamed fish in soy sauce *with* ginger

**SERVES 4**

This is a simple recipe, but there is an exciting element of danger—you will sizzle aromatics in oil and then whiskey, so you have to be careful of flame. It won't be crazy, but whatever happens, it's worth it. The flavor is incredible: You make a 2-minute sauce by seasoning stock with soy sauce and sugar, then pour it and some sizzling ginger over pure steamed fish.

You can use any fish, but I like Chilean sea bass. (The industry has improved its practices and you can find more eco-friendly ones.)

The thinner the ginger the better. But if you don't have good knife skills, I'd rather you have bigger pieces of ginger than the tip of your finger in the food.

I make this the way my favorite restaurant in Trang does. If you have Chinese whiskey, use it because it has such a nice smell. But you can use regular whiskey, too, and have a little for yourself!

### SAUCE

1 cup Chicken Broth (page 146, Nam Soup Gai) or store-bought

½ tablespoon sesame oil

1 tablespoon light brown sugar

1 tablespoon sugar

1 teaspoon to ½ tablespoon kosher salt

½ teaspoon bouillon powder

2 teaspoons Thai black soy sauce

1 tablespoon soy sauce

### STEAMED FISH

1 large or 2 small scallions, halved, and smashed

1 pound Chilean sea bass fillets or any whitefish, skinned, cut into 4 equal pieces

4 tablespoons canola or vegetable oil

4 scallions, cut into thin strips

10 sprigs fresh cilantro

1 red long hot chili, cut into thin strips

2-ounce piece fresh ginger, peeled and cut into matchsticks

3 large garlic cloves, very thinly sliced

1 tablespoon whiskey

1  **Make the sauce:** In a small saucepan, combine the sauce ingredients. Bring to a boil over high heat, stirring frequently; then remove from the heat.

2  **Steam the fish:** Grab your largest, widest steamer, and find a shallow bowl that fits inside the steamer basket or on the steamer rack. Fill the steamer pot with an inch or two of water, not so much that the basket will sit in the water, and set it over high heat.

3  Put the smashed scallion in the shallow bowl. Rub the fish with 1 tablespoon of the oil and set it on top of the scallions.

4  When the water in the steamer pot is boiling, place the bowl with the fish in the steamer basket, lower it into the pot, and cover with a lid. Steam the fish until it's white and firm, about 5 minutes. (If you're using thinner fillets, check after 2 or 3 minutes; you want the fish just cooked.)

5  Carefully remove the bowl from the steamer. Mound the scallion strips, cilantro sprigs, and the chili strips on top of the fish.

6  Bring the sauce back to a boil, then immediately take it off the heat. Pour ½ cup of the sauce around the sides of the bowl with the fish.

7  In a small deep saucepan, heat the remaining 3 tablespoons oil over high heat. When the oil smokes, add the ginger and garlic and cook just until fragrant. Carefully but quickly add the whiskey. Listen to me: Because there is hot oil and alcohol, there is a chance that there will be some flame jumping into the pot. If that happens, don't panic, just stand back and let it burn off and enjoy the excitement. Cook for 15 seconds, then pour the mixture over the fish.

**Serve with:** Jasmine Rice (page 234).

# SOUTHERN HOSPITALITY

When I walked into the space that would be my first restaurant, I could feel in my heart that this was the place. A block away from the Italian market, it could seat thirty with some creativity, it had a kitchen that could be modified for the high-BTU burners I needed, and had exposed brick and blank walls where I could display the work of the strong female artists that I loved. When I first opened my doors, I didn't know what people would say, but I didn't care. It was an opportunity for me to showcase my mother's food and the food of my home.

Those early days were long but exciting. My husband would roll up in his car with Tong, my best friend and best Pomeranian forever, to drop off something I needed, or pick me up after a long shift. Our service was packed, and I was completely exhausted, but every day was so rewarding. I was representing Southern Thai food without apologies, and I could do it my way. There was nothing like Kalaya on the East Coast. The people who tried my food for the first time loved it, and were open to learning, and the people who had a problem, we could work with them to find something they felt safe with. We built a strong base of customers. We started getting press and some award nominations. I started working on collaborations all across the city, even with Italian restaurants.

And then everything shut down. Restaurants workers were out of a job and restaurants suddenly had a backlog of food supply for months and didn't know when it would end.

I did the only thing that I could in that situation. I remembered my mother, who always gave to people, even when she was down on her luck. This time, the whole world seemed down. I remembered our tradition of giving alms in the early morning, of karma, and how life is so cyclical: Things come and go around. We believe in being nice to people.

With the supply of food still sitting in the refrigerators at local restaurants, we acted fast and I started organizing free hot meals for restaurant workers every day, meals they could pick up for themselves and their families. We connected restaurants that didn't know what to do with their inventory and made amazing meals for all the colleagues who felt uncertain about what would happen next. We arranged meals for healthcare and other essential workers, and to anyone who came by, we gave meals, too. We operated like that for a few months.

When outdoor dining resumed, we had to adapt to new rules, new social codes, and new ways of delivering exceptional food, and things were constantly in flux. I innovated with outdoor seating, hosted rotating artists who could sell their work in the streetery space, and felt intrepid and crazy enough to open a Thai market nearby where people could get an easy lunch and some pantry items.

But as the summer went on, things started to work. Eating outside during the summer really felt more like the open-air restaurants of Thailand. We could seat more customers. People were happy just to be out again. There was a learning curve, the wind would blow the umbrellas away . . . and there was that time I hired an eight-piece brass band and all the neighbors were a little mad. But when the hard rain hit the metal roof like a monsoon, and the water came down on the street, my customers stayed warm and dry. People could forget what was happening in the world, and travel without traveling at all, as they shelled a giant river prawn and spooned a hot tom yum soup into their bowls while drinking a glass of wine and looking out onto this beautiful city with new eyes.

In some ways, everything in my upbringing led me to this place. Even though the restaurant is bigger now and we have all come a long way since those difficult times, I still treat everyone who walks through my door like my family. I remember how my mom helped customers in the market while she was being funny and friendly and how meaningful this is to people. One interaction can make a customer's day just by having that human connection. People say sometimes I am like my father, a little reckless, a little impulsive; but I learned customer service and graciousness from my mom. I learned to honor my customers and the products by using the best ingredients and the best methods. People knew about my mom and her personality, in the same way people come to Kalaya because they heard about me and the food. I recently had a customer return to Kalaya for the twenty-ninth time because she just loves it. When I look back, I think of all the memories that we created here, and I feel like I did my job.

# PLA NUNG MANOW

## steamed branzino in spicy broth

SERVES 2 TO 4

Steamed branzino is elegant, and if you have Seafood Sauce (page 34, Nam Jim Seafood) in the fridge, all you have to do is steam the whole fish, pour the sauce over and it will be done in no time. In the first Kalaya restaurant, this was so simple and one of our bestselling dishes. It's a clean-tasting fish, with a tangy, bright, spicy, and beautiful sauce. Fresh chilies, cilantro, and garlic give this a beautiful color, and it is wonderfully healthy. Because this is family-style, everyone can get a taste, but you can also prepare this at home for yourself and your date.

### STEAMED FISH

1 whole branzino (1 pound), cleaned and gutted

Kosher salt and freshly ground black pepper

Ground white pepper

1 tablespoon vegetable oil

1 lemongrass stalk, trimmed and rinsed well

1 sprig fresh cilantro

### BROTH

2 cups Chicken Broth (page 146, Nam Soup Gai) or store-bought

½ to 1 teaspoon kosher salt

1 teaspoon light brown sugar

1 tablespoon fish sauce

½ cup Seafood Sauce (page 34, Nam Jim Seafood)

### FOR SERVING

1 lime, thinly sliced

Handful of fresh cilantro, chopped

¼ cup Seafood Sauce (page 34, Nam Jim Seafood)

1 red long hot chili, thinly sliced

1   Steam the fish: Season the fish liberally with salt, rubbing it on the outside and inside the cavity. Sprinkle lightly with black pepper and white pepper and rub the seasonings on the outside and inside of the fish. Drizzle the oil on top of the fish and rub it in, making sure to get it into the cavity, too. Stuff the cavity of the fish with the lemongrass stalk and cilantro sprig.

2   Fill the bottom of a wide steamer pot with 2 to 3 inches of water and place it over high heat. When the water comes to a boil, lay the fish in the steamer basket and set it in the pot over the water. Cover and let the fish steam until a sharp paring knife can go in and out of the fish without resistance, about 12 minutes. Remove the fish from the steamer.

3   Prepare the broth: When the fish is almost done steaming, pour the chicken broth into a medium pot and bring to a boil over high heat. Stir in the salt, brown sugar, and fish sauce. Remove the pot from the heat and stir in the seafood sauce.

4   To serve: Place the fish in the center of a high-sided oval platter. Pour the broth over the fish, then top it with the lime slices and most of the cilantro. Pour the seafood sauce in a line on top of the fish, and finish by sprinkling with the chili slices and the remaining cilantro. Serve immediately.

# MOO SUB PLA KHEM
## steamed ground pork *with* salted fish & ginger

SERVES 4

This is a confident dish, and the salt and fattiness make you want to eat more rice. This uses a steaming technique that smells lovely. You are making a pork meatloaf with very savory flavors and steaming it until just done and juicy. If "meatloaf" doesn't sound luxurious enough, you can call it "country pâté." You know, pâté is really just meatloaf with good branding.

When I was young, my friend's father would take us to a Chinese restaurant where we could pick from ready-made food that we'd eat with boiled rice. This was the dish I always picked, and I would eat it with fresh raw garlic and chilies. Whenever this is available on the menu, I still order it to this day. It's my favorite.

You can steam this in the oven, too, setting the ramekins with the pork in a roasting pan, wrapped tightly and surrounded by boiling water, and cooking at 350°F.

½ small yellow onion, finely chopped

3 large garlic cloves, finely chopped

1½ tablespoons finely chopped peeled fresh ginger

1 pound ground pork

1 tablespoon sesame oil

1 tablespoon light brown sugar

½ to 1 teaspoon kosher salt

½ tablespoon freshly ground black pepper

½ tablespoon ground white pepper

2 tablespoons soy sauce

1 large egg

3 scallions, thinly sliced

2 tablespoons chopped fresh cilantro

1 large piece jarred salted mackerel in oil, cut into 4 equal pieces, bones removed (or use 4 anchovies)

**FOR SERVING**

Jasmine Rice (page 234)

Fresh ginger, peeled and cut into thin matchsticks

Very thinly sliced long hot chilies

Very thinly sliced scallions

1  In a small food processor, pulse the onion, garlic, and ginger until they are very finely chopped (or mash them together with a mortar and pestle).

2  If you have a large steamer rack, grab it and a wide, deep pot that it will fit inside. If not, grab the largest steamer pot you have. Gather four 6-ounce ramekins or small heatproof bowls, and see if they will fit in your steamer. Don't worry if they won't; you can just work in batches.

3  In a large bowl, combine the onion/garlic/ginger mixture, the ground pork, sesame oil, brown sugar, salt, black pepper, white pepper, soy sauce, egg, scallions, and cilantro. Mix well with your hands. Divide the meat mixture among the ramekins (⅔ cup each) and smooth the tops. Press a piece of salted fish into the top of each ramekin.

4  Pour 2 inches of water into the pot, set the steamer rack or basket in position, and put the pot over high heat.

5  When the water is boiling, arrange the ramekins directly on the rack or in the steamer basket, cover with a lid, and steam until the internal temperature of the ground pork mixture registers 160°F on an instant-read thermometer, about 15 minutes.

6  Serve the steamed pork with rice and thinly sliced ginger, chilies, and scallions.

# GOONG OB WOONSEN
## my mother's acclaimed baked shrimp *with* glass noodles

SERVES 4 TO 6

This is the essential recipe to show how we bake through steam. It cannot be easier than this, and the flavor of shrimp mixes with savory soy sauce, sugar, plenty of black and white pepper, ginger, and nutty sesame oil. Chinese celery adds a big aroma, and all this soaks into light and bouncy glass noodles. You won't want to stop eating it. The evaporated milk used here makes the flavor mellow. This recipe is delicious, but I have to tell you that when we did the blind test, my mom's version is much better than mine. We all have to keep learning!

Cut the noodles before you cook them and flip the shrimp on the top so you don't overcook it. Also, Chinese celery is much thinner and has a much stronger aroma than Western celery. If you can't find it, add some of the leaves from a standard bunch of celery.

### NOODLES AND SAUCE

5 ounces glass noodles

½ cup evaporated milk

5 tablespoons soy sauce

2 tablespoons Thai black soy sauce

1 tablespoon sesame oil

½ teaspoon freshly ground black pepper

½ teaspoon ground white pepper

1½ tablespoons light brown sugar

2 tablespoons very thinly sliced peeled fresh ginger (1½- to 2-ounce piece)

5 large garlic cloves, roughly chopped

### STEAM-BAKED SHRIMP

1 pound extra-large shrimp, deveined, shells left on

6 scallions, cut into 1-inch pieces

1 large stalk Chinese celery, roughly chopped, plus a handful of chopped celery leaves

1½ red long hot chilies, sliced on the diagonal

Seafood Sauce (page 34, Nam Jim Seafood), for serving

1   Prepare the noodles and sauce: Put the glass noodles in a large bowl and cover with hot tap water. Let soak for 12 minutes, or until they begin to soften. Drain well and snip them through a few times with scissors.

2   In a medium bowl, whisk together the evaporated milk, ¼ cup water, the regular soy sauce, black soy sauce, sesame oil, black pepper, white pepper, and brown sugar. Mix in the ginger and garlic.

3   Cook the shrimp: Put the shrimp in a heavy medium pot in a single layer. Put the soaked and drained glass noodles on top of the shrimp, spreading them out in an even layer. Put the scallions, chopped celery stalk, and all but 7 or 8 slices of chili on top. Finally, pour in the prepared sauce.

4   Set the pot over high heat and cover with a lid. Cook until the sauce is bubbling, about 3 minutes. Use tongs to stir the noodles and bring the shrimp onto the top, flipping the shrimp cooked-side up. Add the reserved chilies and the celery leaves. Cover and cook just until the shrimp are opaque and the noodles have absorbed the sauce, about 2 minutes more.

5   Divide among bowls and serve with the seafood sauce.

# GOONG OB KLUER

## my mother's 5-minute baked shrimp *with* salt

**SERVES 4 TO 6**

My niece Nong Noon loves this dish. When my mom would make it, and Nong Noon was a small girl, she would peel the shrimp and stuff her face with the big prawns. This is very easy and will be complete in under 10 minutes. The technique is between a sear and a steam; you are just searing the shrimp (shells on, please, for flavor) in a pan, but adding a splash of water to create steam, which cooks the shrimp more quickly and evenly.

1 pound jumbo shrimp (the largest you can get), deveined, shells left on

2 tablespoons canola or vegetable oil

1½ to 2 teaspoons kosher salt

Pinch of freshly ground black pepper

Pinch of ground white pepper

In a large bowl, toss the shrimp with the oil, salt, black pepper, and white pepper. Put the seasoned shrimp in a heavy medium lidded pan with 2 tablespoons water and set over high heat. Cover the pan and cook for 3 minutes. Flip the shrimp, cover the pan, turn off the heat, and let the shrimp sit just until opaque, about 2 more minutes.

# HOI MANG PHU OB SAMUN PRAI

## baked mussels *with* herbs

SERVES 4 TO 6

The market we grew up in had everything you could ask for, and my mother would be able to make the most beautiful meals from everything in the market and the garden. When we had mussels, which are so quick and easy to cook, she would simply bake the mussels in a pot on the stove with herbs like basil, lime leaves, and lemongrass, until they open and release their own juice. The herbs infuse the mussels, which cook in about five minutes. These mussels paired with a spicy seafood sauce are the perfect luxury. Pour yourself a glass of cold beer. Cheers!

2 pounds fresh mussels

1 large bunch basil, leaves picked

5 makrut lime leaves, torn

1 lemongrass stalk, trimmed and smashed with the side of a large knife

1 large shallot, halved and smashed with the side of a large knife

5 large garlic cloves, smashed with the side of a large knife

1 tablespoon canola oil

Seafood Sauce (page 34, Nam Jim Seafood), for serving

1   Rinse the mussels really well under cold running water, discarding any that have open or cracked shells. Place the mussels in a large bowl and top with the basil leaves, lime leaves, lemongrass, shallot, and garlic.

2   In a large pot, heat the oil over high heat. When the oil begins to smoke, add the mussels and aromatics to the pot and cover with a lid. Cook just until the mussels all open. This could take 2 minutes, it could take 5, or a few more. Open the lid to peek and stir once a minute or so. If there are a couple of stubborn unopened ones, discard them rather than overcook the rest of the mussels while waiting for them. If you want to be fussy, you can take out the open mussels to prevent them from cooking more while you wait for the rest.

3   Immediately transfer the mussels and aromatics to a platter. Serve with the seafood sauce.

# MOO HONG
## braised pork belly

Moo hong is a stew and a Southern comfort food. *Hong* is a Chinese word that means "stew," though the accent is different in Thai. And *moo* just means "pork" in Thai, but I always make this with skin-on pork belly. Skin-on for the pork adds a thickness and a natural collagen. You want the sauce to be thick and creamy, and the skin helps you get there.

Sometimes customers ask me "Can I have pork belly without fat?" and I say "No, you can't. Don't be afraid of the fat. It will make you happy." Remember fat and sweet always work together, and this is a combination of meat, palm sugar, sweet garlic, shallots, soy sauce, and some vinegar to add a fresh pop. The homemade five-spice powder makes it so warm and fragrant, and you will have a beautiful bubbling pot of braised pork on your stove.

It takes a while to make, so this recipe is a pretty big one to have leftovers.

¼ cup canola oil

10 large garlic cloves, smashed with the side of a large knife

2 large shallots, halved and thinly sliced

2 inches of stems and the roots (see Note) from 1 bunch cilantro, rinsed well and chopped (¼ to ⅓ cup)

3 (70g) discs palm sugar or ¾ cup brown sugar

2 tablespoons Five-Spice Powder (page 59)

5 star anise pods

3 cinnamon sticks

1½ pounds skin-on pork belly, cut into 2-inch pieces

2 tablespoons Thai black soy sauce

5 tablespoons soy sauce

1 teaspoon freshly ground black pepper

1 teaspoon ground white pepper

1  In a large, heavy pot, heat the oil over medium heat. Add the garlic, shallots, cilantro stems, and palm sugar and cook, stirring frequently, until the palm sugar melts, 2 to 5 minutes (this will vary depending on the form of palm sugar you have). Increase the heat to high and stir in the five-spice powder, star anise, and cinnamon sticks. Cook for 30 seconds to 1 minute, until very fragrant.

2  Add the pork belly, black soy sauce, regular soy sauce, black pepper, and white pepper. Stir well and cook, stirring frequently, until the sauce is thick and caramelized, 1 to 2 minutes. Pour in 7 cups water and bring to a boil. Reduce the heat to a slow simmer and cook until the pork belly is jiggly and tender, 1 to 1½ hours.

3  Increase the heat to high and bring the liquid to a boil. Cook, stirring frequently, until the liquid has reduced to a syrupy consistency. The amount of time varies, depending on how much the water has reduced in your pot, but it could take up to 30 to 40 minutes.

**Serve with:** Jasmine Rice (page 234).

**Note:** If you can't find cilantro roots, just use all chopped stems.

# MEAL MAKERS

**If you think about the most enjoyable meal you've ever had, it probably includes a recipe that brought it together by marrying flavors: a tangy mango chutney paired with a roti and curry, a Nordic mustard-cream sauce for salmon, or a salsa verde for your taco.**

There are food memories that are so strong, not because of any one individual dish, but because of recipes that work in partnership together. Rice and beans; pierogi, fried onions, and sour cream; fresh pita and a beautiful mezze. Sure, you could eat them alone, but that would be sad, and there would always be something missing.

In Thailand, eggs, rice, lhon and tom krati (both types of dips or gravy), and nam prik (relishes) are the recipes that offer a meal that sense of completeness.

The rice recipes here are the ones that your friends will keep asking about, from my golden Turmeric Fried Rice (page 236, Khao Pad Kamin) and the Green Coconut Rice (page 235) to your new family favorite, Khao Pad Pu (page 238, Egg and Crab Fried Rice). Of course, I will show you my method for perfect jasmine rice and sticky rice, too.

Our eggs are stylish, with beautiful drapes and folds paired with colorful vegetables and dipping sauces like in Khai Yud Saai (page 251, Pi Goong's and Pi Kul's Stuffed Egg Crepes) or paired with canned crab like Khai Jiew Pu (page 246, Nok's Lifesaving Crabmeat Omelet), and its vegetarian cousin, Khai Jiew Samoun Prai (page 249, Cilantro, Basil, and Scallion Omelet), recipes that you will find yourself going back to on your best cooking days and your worst. For us, we will add even a simple plain omelet—we cook it in a unique way to get it very savory—to the table anytime; with rice and whatever else you have, it will make a satisfying meal. Remember, when life gets you down, just add an omelet using one of the omelet recipes above, without any fillings.

And the lhon and tom krati recipes are the showstopping mild and savory gravies and dips that serve as a palate cleanser and make you want to eat more. Lhon Pu (page 262, Coconut Crab Gravy) and Nam Prik Saparot (page 258, Pineapple Chili Paste) shine with raw vegetables or serve as a kind of between-bite companion to your meal.

Make any of these recipes in addition to a stir-fry, curry, or braise, and you have made a beautiful and exciting dinner. On those impossibly jam-packed days, you can even just add any one of these recipes to rice and your meal will be complete and satisfying. If you can't make a decision, you can make one recipe from each section and keep them in the fridge until you need them. This chapter holds the missing pieces of your Southern Thai feast puzzle. When you feel lost in your kitchen, when you feel nervous, this is the chapter you open to in this book and get cooking.

## Rice
### Khao

I don't need to tell you that rice is our life. In Thailand, when we greet each other, we always ask "Gin khao mai?" which translates to "Have you eaten rice today?" Rice is an economic livelihood for Thai people; in Southern Thailand there are 162 types of rice, and Thailand remains one of the largest rice producers in the world. It is sacred in Thai culture; rice has a soul, and it is the foundation of everything we do. There is a way to bring out the flavor, the cadence, and the fragrance of a good crop of rice. But you don't need the perfect crop of rice to have an outstanding meal. If rice is given the proper respect in both cooking and eating, the meal will be that much more delicious. Well-made rice has a satisfying, chewy texture and a sweet, mellow flavor that goes with almost any dish or relish. When you cook these recipes, remember rice is anything but basic.

# JASMINE RICE

**SERVES 4**

Do not underestimate the power of a pot of perfectly cooked jasmine rice. Through all the joys and challenges in life, rice will always reassure you. Having a glass lid for your pot may help, so you are not tempted to lift the lid while the rice cooks if you're not yet confident. But trust yourself, trust your rice. Leave your pot covered! A nonstick pot can be useful but not necessary. A rice cooker is how most Asian people make rice at home, but if you have a rice cooker, then you don't need me to tell you how to use it.

2 cups jasmine rice

1  Add the rice to a medium saucepan or small pot in your kitchen sink. Fill the pan a little more than halfway with cool tap water, swish the rice around with your hand, and then carefully tip the pan to pour out the cloudy water without losing the rice. Repeat this process two or three more times, until the water stays mostly clear.

2  Pour enough cool tap water into the pan to cover the rice by 1 inch. If you don't feel like taking out a ruler, dip your index finger into the water until it touches the top of the rice; the water should come up to your first knuckle.

3  Put the pan over high heat and bring the water to a bubble. Let the rice boil for a few minutes, until there is only a little bit of water on top, then cover the pan with a tight-fitting lid (preferably glass, so you can watch the rice as it cooks) and reduce the heat to low. Cook without lifting the lid until all the water is absorbed and the rice is tender, about 15 minutes.

4  Turn off the heat and let the rice sit for at least 5 minutes. Fluff with a fork or spoon before serving.

# GREEN COCONUT RICE

**SERVES 4**

I created this recipe based on memories of my great-grandmother's sweet and aromatic coconut rice. The cilantro and pandan leaf give the rice its elegant green color and combined with coconut milk, the rice has a smooth herbaceous flavor. Green coconut rice with pandan leaf was rarely seen in the United States until I served it at Kalaya, but now I am seeing green rice on social media more often. I like to think I started the trend! This rice can be paired with a wide variety of curries, including Green Curry with Beef Shanks (page 127, Gaeng Kiew Waan Osso Buco), but its delicate and herby sweetness complements chicken curry beautifully.

5 pandan leaves (see Note), roughly chopped

1 bunch fresh cilantro (4 ounces)

4 ounces (½ cup plus 1 tablespoon) sugar

2 tablespoons kosher salt

3 cups jasmine rice, rinsed in a sieve until the water runs very clear

1 (13.5-ounce) can coconut milk

6 garlic cloves, smashed with the side of a knife and peeled

¾ cup thinly sliced shallots

1 In a blender or food processor, combine 4 cups water, the pandan leaves, cilantro, sugar, and salt. Puree until smooth and uniform in color.

2 Transfer the rinsed rice and pandan/cilantro liquid to a large nonstick pot. Stir in the coconut milk, garlic, and shallots.

3 Bring the mixture to a boil over high heat. Reduce the heat to medium-low, cover, and cook for 7 minutes. Stir the rice with a fork, re-cover, and cook for 8 more minutes. Stir again with a fork, re-cover, reduce the heat to low, and cook until the rice is tender and the liquid is absorbed, about 5 more minutes. Fluff one more time with a fork before serving.

**NOTE:** If you don't have pandan, you can add 2 more loosely packed cups cilantro leaves and tender stems, instead. It's a totally different flavor, but will be good.

# STICKY RICE

SERVES 2

Rice is life, and in its purest form, it complements many other flavors and has its own special nuance. Sticky rice, which is popular all over Thailand, clumps together easily and has a very satisfying chewiness.

You can have sticky rice with anything, but pairing it with grilled proteins and roasted pork is exceptional. In Thailand we keep it in small bamboo steamer baskets, so it doesn't dry out. As soon as you are done cooking it, put it in an airtight container.

When shopping for it, be sure you are buying "sticky" rice, not just short-grain or sushi rice, which sometimes confuses people. It is often labeled glutinous rice, but don't worry, it doesn't actually contain gluten. Your cousin in LA can still eat it.

You can revive leftover refrigerated sticky rice with a few drops of water and microwave it for 30 seconds, but it's best eaten fresh.

| | |
|---|---|
| 1 cup sticky rice (aka sweet or glutinous rice) | Cooking spray, for the steamer basket |
| | 1 cup hot water |

1   Soak the rice in a bowl of cold water overnight at room temperature. Drain the rice when you're ready to cook.

2   Bring a few inches of water to a boil in a steamer pot over high heat. Coat the inside of a steamer basket with cooking spray or line it with damp cheesecloth, then add the drained rice. When the water is boiling, set the steamer basket on top and fold the cheesecloth (if using) over the rice. Cover and steam until the rice is tender, about 6 minutes.

3   Pour the hot water over the rice, stir, then cover and steam for another 3 minutes, or until tender but chewy. (You will have to add more time if you are making more rice.)

4   Put in a bowl and cover it, because sticky rice dries out fast.

# KHAO PAD KAMIN
## turmeric fried rice

SERVES 2 TO 4

Once you make the turmeric paste and put it in the freezer, you can use it anytime to marinate meats for grilling, but I love to use it to flavor an easy fried rice. It's magical with the balance of turmeric and pepper, and the sweet from the brown sugar to balance the heat. Rice is versatile and there are so many ways to enjoy it, but this adds a visual beauty to a meal with its beautiful golden color. I love eating this with simple fried eggs, as part of a large spread, or especially with Oxtail Soup (page 157, Soup Hang Wua); its earthiness goes so well with the rich beef flavor of that dish.

| | |
|---|---|
| 2 cups cooked Jasmine Rice (page 234), cold or room temperature | ½ to 1 teaspoon kosher salt |
| 1 teaspoon plus 2 tablespoons canola oil | 2 teaspoons light brown sugar |
| | ¼ cup Turmeric Paste (page 55) |
| 2 tablespoons soy sauce | 1 tablespoon minced garlic |

1   In a large bowl, mix together the rice, 1 teaspoon of the oil, the soy sauce, salt, brown sugar, and turmeric paste with your hands, separating the rice to make sure there aren't any lumps.

2   In a heavy wok or Dutch oven, heat the remaining 2 tablespoons oil over high heat until smoking. Add the rice mixture. Spread it out, make a well in the center, and add the garlic to the well. Cook until the garlic is fragrant, about 30 seconds.

3   Stir together and spread out the rice, let it cook until the rice starts to pop and dance, and then stir, scraping any stuck-on bits from the bottom of the pot. Repeat for about 3 minutes, until the rice is starting to brown. Serve.

# KHAO PAD PU
## egg & crab fried rice

**SERVES 4**

This fried rice is so delicious, and it takes under 10 minutes to make. Here is a secret: Premix the seasonings in the rice and make sure it's not lumpy. Then stir-fry the egg first in the pan—make sure you cook the egg until fragrant—and your rice will never be mushy.

If you want your family to be happy, this easy fried rice really pops. It's not overly sweet and it's perfectly comforting and balanced. Let the rice dance and you know you are doing things right!

If you get a wok, get a good solid wok (one that lasts longer than a marriage). The wok helps because you can really toss and mix the rice with all that room. But otherwise, I suggest a heavy Dutch oven instead of a skillet, because that gives you more space to work with.

1  **Season the rice:** In a large bowl, gently mix together the rice, soy sauce, black pepper, white pepper, salt, brown sugar, and sesame oil with your hands, separating the rice to prevent clumps.

2  **Cook the eggs:** In a large heavy wok or Dutch oven, heat the oil over medium-high heat until smoking. Add the eggs, salt, black pepper, and white pepper and cook, stirring with a wooden spoon or spatula, until the egg is scrambled.

3  Make a well in the center by pushing the egg to the sides of the pan. Add the garlic and onion to the well and cook, stirring, until the onion is translucent, about 1 minute.

4  Make another well in the center and add the seasoned rice and cook, spreading out the rice, letting it dance in the skillet, then stirring, until the rice begins to brown and is very hot, 2 to 4 minutes.

5  Make a well again and add the scallions and crabmeat. Cook, stirring, for about 1 more minute, until the scallion is bright green and the crab is heated through.

**Serve with:** Fish Sauce and Chili Condiment (page 42, Prik Nam Pla) or Seafood Sauce (page 34, Nam Jim Seafood).

### SEASONED RICE

2 cups cooked Jasmine Rice (page 234), cold

1 tablespoon soy sauce

¼ teaspoon freshly ground black pepper

¼ teaspoon ground white pepper

½ teaspoon kosher salt

1 teaspoon light brown sugar

1 teaspoon sesame oil

### EGGS

¼ cup canola oil

3 large eggs

½ to 1 teaspoon kosher salt

Pinch of freshly ground black pepper

Pinch of ground white pepper

3 large garlic cloves, chopped

½ cup finely chopped white onion

1 cup chopped scallion (10 to 12 medium scallions)

1 cup canned crabmeat (I love jumbo lump or colossal, but use what you like!)

# KHAO NIEW LUANG NAH GOONG

## yellow sticky rice *with* shrimp

At Southern Thai weddings you will eat this turmeric-coconut sticky rice because the golden color is so lucky. The symbolism of yellow is for prosperity, and adding a delicate layer of stir-fried coconut and minced shrimp and a coconut cream sauce feels so fancy.

The sticky rice you have should be warm, not hot (or it will get too soggy) and not cold. It's a bit of work, but so worth it. The strong sweet-salty taste makes you want more.

Present it in individual portions as written here and everyone will be dazzled, or put it all in a bowl and eat in front of the TV. Maybe watch some sports and make some bets. I won't tell.

### RICE

2 cups coconut milk

1 tablespoon ground turmeric

⅔ cup granulated sugar

1½ to 2 teaspoons kosher salt

Sticky Rice (page 236), still warm (but not hot)

### SHRIMP

1 pound jumbo shrimp, peeled and deveined

5 large garlic cloves, finely chopped

2 tablespoons cilantro stems

1 tablespoon freshly ground black pepper

1 tablespoon ground white pepper

½ to 1 teaspoon kosher salt

¼ cup vegetable oil

1 cup unsweetened coconut flakes

3 (70g) discs palm sugar or ¾ cup brown sugar

¼ cup Ground Dried Shrimp (page 137)

3 drops orange food coloring

1 tablespoon fish sauce

1 tablespoon finely sliced makrut lime leaves

¼ cup chopped fresh cilantro leaves

### SAUCE

1½ cups coconut cream

2 tablespoons rice flour

1 tablespoon kosher salt

1 **Prepare the rice:** In a medium saucepan, combine the coconut milk, turmeric, granulated sugar, and salt. Cook over high heat, stirring, until the coconut milk comes to a boil, then remove it from the heat.

2 Put the cooked rice in a large heatproof bowl and pour the hot coconut milk mixture over top. It will look soupy—do not panic. Cover the bowl with plastic wrap or a lid and set aside for 5 minutes. Stir the rice, smooth it out, then cover it again and let it sit for 5 more minutes. Stir well.

3 **Cook the shrimp:** In a food processor, combine the shrimp, garlic, cilantro stems, black pepper, white pepper, and salt and pulse until the shrimp is roughly chopped.

4 Set a wok over high heat, pour in the oil and immediately add the coconut flakes. Cook, stirring, until the coconut is fragrant and golden brown, about 1 minute. The coconut will soak up the oil, then release it again. Add the shrimp mixture to the wok and reduce the heat to medium. Stir in ¾ cup water, then make a well in the center of the wok. Put the palm sugar in the well and cook until the palm sugar melts. Add the ground dried shrimp, food coloring, fish sauce, lime leaves, and cilantro and stir everything together. Remove from the heat.

5 **Make the sauce:** In a small saucepan, whisk together the coconut cream, rice flour, and salt. Cook over medium heat, whisking constantly, until thickened. Remove from the heat and set aside.

6 Put the shrimp mixture into small bowls and top with yellow sticky rice. Press down and flatten the rice, then invert onto small appetizer plates (or larger plates if you're eating this as an entrée). Spoon some of the sauce over top and serve.

# KRU PADUNG

I will never stop learning, and you shouldn't either. Every time I visit Thailand, I spend time learning from Kru Padung.

*Kru* means "teacher" in Thai, and Kru Padung interviewed me before I could train as his student. He believed in me, and believed in what I was doing to represent Thai food in America. His family has cooked Royal Thai food for over a century, and the flavors, the presentation, and the ingredients are time-honored and true. He has been learning the ancient recipes from his great-grandmother since he was ten years old.

He is both serious and funny, warm but firm. To learn from him and share these recipes means that they won't get lost. The ancient recipes will be shared with a new audience, and they will continue to evolve over time. The way he uses subtle flavor and presents his food is so precise and beautiful. I learn different tricks from him, and he is constantly challenging me to use ingredients in ways that are new to me, like adding lime leaf to toasted rice powder to add an extra layer of fragrance. It's so simple and yet adds so much dimension to a recipe.

The way we cook and our food memories are different. Just like your pizza and tacos are different across regions of America, our regional food varies in Thailand. And when I learn from Kru Padung, it's not just regional difference, it's different because he knows the food and tastes of royalty. Kru Padung's flavors are delicate and bright, he will not use freshly ground white pepper because he says the flavor is too strong, but in my family, we have a very heavy hand with white pepper. But our goals are the same, we are trying to showcase the heritage of our recipes, our culture, and our way of life.

When Kru Padung uses flavor in different ways, it reminds me that everyone has a different flavor of hand, and everyone can adjust those flavors to their liking. After I learn from him, I cannot wait to go back to the restaurant and develop new recipes and share these techniques with the world

For me and Kru Padung, even though the ingredients, the process of cooking, and the seasonings may change slightly over the years, our love of the food and our family recipes are still the same. Our passion for showing the brightest and best dishes will always be there, as well as our hope to carry these recipes on and introduce them to a new generation.

## Khai
### Eggs

Most problems in life can be solved by adding an egg. Whether it's a beautifully styled omelet or a puffy fried egg, you have instant nutrition, comfort, and flavor. Eggs are not just for breakfast in most of the world. We must get over the way certain foods are thought to be only for a certain time of day. I come from a culture of breakfast all day, where rich sweet protein is served for breakfast, and beautiful, spiced, savory eggs can be served for dinner. These delicious flavors don't run on a schedule. The recipes in this section showcase the ingredients at the greatest potential. They are satisfying, flavorful, and an all-day crowd-pleaser.

# KHAI PA LO HED
## five-spice egg & mushrooms *with* tofu

SERVES 4 TO 6

This is my childhood comfort food and is so kid friendly. Once your kid loves it, you will love it, too. If you are not vegetarian you can add pork and it will be another one-pot wonder.

5 large eggs

¼ cup canola oil

2 large shallots, sliced

¼ cup chopped cilantro

10 large garlic cloves, chopped

3 (70g) discs palm sugar or ¾ cup brown sugar

2 tablespoons Thai black soy sauce

5 tablespoons soy sauce

5 star anise pods

1 tablespoon Five-Spice Powder (page 59)

3 cinnamon sticks

1 tablespoon kosher salt

½ teaspoon freshly ground black pepper

½ teaspoon ground white pepper

2 (7-ounce) packages fried cubed bean curd (see Note)

4 large dried shiitake mushrooms, soaked, liquid reserved (see page 25)

1 In a medium saucepan, combine the eggs with enough lukewarm water to cover them and set the pan over high heat. As soon as the water begins to boil, remove the pan from the heat and set a timer for 10 minutes. Fill a large bowl with ice water while you wait. When the timer goes off, transfer the eggs to the bowl of ice water and let them cool completely. Peel them and set them aside on a plate.

2 In a large pot, heat the oil over high heat. Add the shallots, cilantro, garlic, and palm sugar. Cook, stirring frequently, until the palm sugar has fully melted, 2 to 5 minutes.

3 Stir in the black soy sauce, regular soy sauce, star anise, five-spice powder, cinnamon sticks, salt, black pepper, and white pepper. Add the peeled hard-boiled eggs, fried bean curd, mushrooms, 2 cups mushroom soaking liquid, and 4 cups water. Bring to a boil, reduce the heat to medium, and cook for at least 1 hour or up to 2 hours. The longer it cooks, the more flavorful it will be.

NOTE: You can find packages of fried cubes of bean curd (tofu) in most any East Asian or Southeast Asian grocery store.

# KHAI JIEW PU
## nok's lifesaving crabmeat omelet

Holy crab! I'm about to change your life again. This omelet is satisfying, healthy, and shows exactly why you need to keep canned crab in the fridge.

No matter what the European chefs say, no one likes a flat and floppy omelet. This Thai technique for making omelets is like a cross between a frittata and a soufflé; everybody deserves light and fluffy eggs with a beautiful brown crust. Flavored with soy sauce and scallions, this is a one-plate meal with rice, or it can be served family-style with everyone taking a piece. Serve it with sriracha or Sweet Chili Sauce (page 41).

You might think this recipe uses a lot of oil. Don't tell me there is too much oil . . . don't second-guess the oil. We are Team Oil. The eggs puff up in this technique because the hot oil forces the steam to fluff the eggs up as they cook—and the steam pushes the excess oil out from the top.

And the technique of flipping the omelet is fun and educational. You bought this book so you could learn something, so you'll enjoy mastering the flip technique, and you'll enjoy how the egg soufflés up.

5 large eggs

8 ounces (1 heaping cup) crabmeat (of course, I love jumbo lump)

½ cup thinly sliced scallions

1 teaspoon fresh lime juice

2 tablespoons soy sauce

Pinch of kosher salt

Pinch of freshly ground black pepper

Pinch of ground white pepper

½ cup canola or vegetable oil

Sriracha, ketchup, or Sweet Chili Sauce (page 41), for serving

Jasmine Rice (page 234), for serving

1 Crack the eggs into a large bowl and whisk them until smooth. Stir in the crabmeat, scallions, lime juice, soy sauce, salt, black pepper, and white pepper.

2 Set a 7- or 8-inch sauté pan or small saucepan (preferably nonstick) over high heat. Let it preheat for 2 minutes or so, then pour in the oil. While the oil heats up, grab a small heatproof bowl (for excess oil) and a small skillet (for flipping the omelet), and line a plate with paper towels.

3 Pour the egg mixture into the pan with the hot oil, still over high heat. When the edges have set, after a minute or so, use a silicone spatula to push the cooked egg from the edges to the middle, letting the uncooked egg flow to the bottom of the pan. Poke a hole in the center of the egg, too, so any uncooked egg can run to the bottom. Keep cooking like this, pressing inward from around the edges and poking holes in the center, for about 4 minutes, until the edges of the omelet feel firm.

4 Invert the small skillet over the omelet. Then flip the pans together so the omelet lands in the skillet. Then slide the omelet, browned-side up, back into the pan. Cook until the bottom is browned, about 2 minutes, pressing in around the edges and down from the top. When you see oil pooling in the bottom of the pan, press it out into the heatproof bowl and keep cooking. Flip the omelet one more time, using the skillet. Then slide it back into the pan and poke a hole in the center of the omelet to let any remaining uncooked egg flow to the bottom. Cook over high heat for 1 to 2 more minutes, pressing on the omelet from all sides to release as much oil as you can. Carefully pour the oil into the heatproof bowl, and transfer the omelet to the paper towels to drain.

5 Serve with sriracha sauce, ketchup, or sweet chili sauce, and rice.

# KHAI JIEW SAMOUN PRAI

## cilantro, basil & scallion omelet

SERVES 4 TO 6

This vegetarian dish uses a similar technique to the Nok's Lifesaving Crabmeat Omelet (page 246, Khai Jiew Pu) for a fluffy, browned omelet that is delicious with rice.

6 large eggs

Pinch to ½ teaspoon
  kosher salt

2 tablespoons soy sauce

2 tablespoons coconut
  cream or coconut milk

½ teaspoon freshly
  ground black pepper

½ teaspoon ground
  white pepper

½ cup basil leaves

1 large shallot, halved
  and very thinly sliced
  (about ½ cup)

¼ cup finely chopped
  scallions

2 tablespoons finely
  chopped fresh cilantro

½ cup canola or
  vegetable oil

Sriracha sauce or
  ketchup, for serving

1   In a large bowl, whisk together the eggs, salt, soy sauce, coconut cream, black pepper, and white pepper with a fork. Add the basil leaves, shallot, scallions, and cilantro and stir gently until everything is evenly distributed.

2   Set a 7- or 8-inch sauté pan or small saucepan (preferably nonstick) over high heat. Let it preheat for 2 minutes or so, then pour in the oil. While the oil heats up, grab a small heatproof bowl (for excess oil) and a small skillet (for flipping the omelet), and line a plate with paper towels.

3   Pour the egg mixture into the pan with the hot oil, still over high heat. When the edges have set, after a minute or so, use a silicone spatula to push the cooked egg from the edges to the middle, letting the uncooked egg flow to the bottom of the pan. Poke a hole in the center of the egg, too, so any uncooked egg can run to the bottom. Keep cooking like this, pressing inward from around the edges and poking holes in the center, for about 4 minutes, until the edges of the omelet feel firm.

4   Invert the small skillet over the omelet, flip the pans together so the omelet lands in the skillet; then slide the omelet, browned-side up, back into the pan. Cook until the bottom is browned, about 2 minutes, pressing in around the edges and down from the top. When you see oil pooling in the bottom of the pan, press it out into the heatproof bowl and keep cooking. Flip the omelet one more time, using the skillet. Then slide it back into the pan and poke a hole in the center of the omelet to let any remaining uncooked egg flow to the bottom. Cook over high heat for 1 to 2 more minutes, pressing on the omelet from all sides to release as much oil as you can. Carefully pour the oil into the heatproof bowl, and transfer the omelet to the paper towels to drain.

5   Serve with sriracha sauce or ketchup.

# KHAI YUD SAAI

## pi goong's & pi kul's stuffed egg crepes

My cousins Pi Goong, Pi Kul, and I grew up together. Pi Goong and Pi Kul always loved and cared for me, and Pi Goong doesn't like spicy food. This is their go-to dish. No matter how far we are apart, when we come together it's like time never passed and this is the dish that they will always make. This is a perfect way to showcase the elegance of a simple egg. And what a great recipe to sneak some vegetables into your meal while improving your focus, because the folding of the omelet requires some technique. The key is to make sure there is no extra liquid in the filling, so you drain the meat well and pay attention to the amount of filling because folding can be a little tricky. Make sure the edges are airy and thin, and the center is strong enough to hold the filling. When it is complete, open the eggs like a little parcel so people can admire your hard work.

This technique takes a little practice because stuffed egg crepes are very delicate, but the messy ones are delicious, too!

### FILLING

¼ cup canola or vegetable oil

3 garlic cloves, chopped

½ pound ground pork

1 teaspoon Thai black soy sauce

1 teaspoon soy sauce

½ cup peas and carrots

½ cup finely chopped onion

¼ cup chopped scallions

2 tablespoons finely chopped fresh cilantro

½ teaspoon freshly ground black pepper

½ teaspoon ground white pepper

1 tablespoon light brown sugar

Pinch to ½ teaspoon kosher salt

### EGG CREPES

4 large eggs

1 teaspoon canola or vegetable oil, plus more for cooking

Kosher salt

Freshly ground black pepper

Ground white pepper

Fish sauce

1 **Make the filling:** In a large skillet, heat the oil over high heat. Add the garlic and ground pork and cook, breaking up the pork into small pieces until the meat is browned. Add the black soy sauce, regular soy sauce, peas and carrots, onion, scallions, cilantro, black pepper, white pepper, brown sugar, and salt. Cook for a couple minutes, just until the pork is well browned and the onion is translucent. Pour the mixture into a colander set over a bowl to drain off the fat and excess liquid.

2 **Make the egg crepes:** In a small bowl, whisk 2 of the eggs with ½ teaspoon of the oil, a pinch each of salt, black pepper, and white pepper, and a splash of fish sauce. Repeat with the remaining eggs, oil, and seasonings in a second small bowl.

3 Grab a heatproof bowl or ramekin and put it near the stove. In a large wok or a nonstick skillet, heat a few glugs of oil over high heat. When the oil is smoking, quickly swirl it around the wok to coat the pan, pour the oil into the heatproof bowl, and set the wok back on the burner.

4 Reduce the heat to medium. Then immediately pour the egg mixture from one of the bowls into the hot wok, tilting the pan to swirl the egg mixture into one large, thin crepe. It won't look perfect on your first try; don't worry! Drizzle some of the reserved oil down around the edges of the wok to help loosen the egg. Spoon half of the meat mixture onto the center of the egg crepe and use a thin spatula to fold the egg up and over the filling like an envelope. Again: Don't stress. If your first one doesn't look perfect, you'll get it on the next try. Carefully slide the stuffed egg crepe onto a plate and cover it with foil.

5 Repeat to cook a second egg crepe with the second bowl of egg mixture and filling.

**Serve with:** Sriracha sauce or ketchup.

# KHAI TOON MOO SUB

## steamed eggs *with* ground pork & salted egg yolk

**SERVES 4 TO 6**

There is an egg custard in every Asian culture. In Japan, they have chawanmushi—a savory pudding made with eggs and dashi. In Korean barbecue restaurants, sometimes you will see a little moat of eggs steaming next to the grill.

In Trang, we do a double-egg: We steam eggs mixed with seasoned pork and put salted egg yolk, a kind of preserved yolk that is very savory, in the center. If you steam it low and slow, it will look like a soufflé and then when you add the beautiful salted egg yolk, it looks like sunshine on a cloud. Every bite should be scooped with a spoon and have a little bit of everything and goes great with rice.

If the amount of salted egg yolk you find at the Asian grocery store is more than you need to use, don't worry. In the freezer, the salted eggs last longer than you and I put together.

½ pound ground pork

½ tablespoon canola oil

1 tablespoon soy sauce

½ to 1 teaspoon kosher salt

1 tablespoon light brown sugar

1 teaspoon freshly ground black pepper

1 teaspoon ground white pepper

2 tablespoons fish sauce

5 large eggs, whisked together

¼ cup chopped fresh cilantro

3 scallions, thinly sliced

5 salted egg yolks

¼ cup Fried Garlic (page 45)

1 tablespoon garlic oil (page 45)

Jasmine Rice (page 234), for serving

1 In a large bowl, combine the pork, oil, soy sauce, salt, brown sugar, black pepper, white pepper, fish sauce, and eggs. Mix with a fork until the meat is broken down into very small pieces. Pour in 2 cups water, the cilantro, and scallions and mix with your hands until the pork is in even smaller pieces and everything is evenly incorporated.

2 Set up a wide steamer pot over high heat. If you're using a steamer rack, set it inside the pot now; if you have a large steamer basket, set it aside. Find a wide heatproof bowl, pie plate, or cake pan that fits in your steamer pot.

3 Pour the egg and pork mixture into the heatproof bowl or pan. When the water boils in the steamer, carefully set the bowl or pan on the rack, or set it in your steamer basket and lower it into the pot. Cover with a lid, reduce the heat to medium-low, and steam until the egg/pork mixture puffs up a bit, about 15 minutes.

4 Uncover and press the salted egg yolks into the top of the steamed eggs. Cover and steam until the center of the custard is firm, 12 to 15 more minutes.

5 Remove from the steamer and top with the fried garlic and garlic oil. Serve with jasmine rice.

## Lhon, Tom Krati, and Nam Prik

If you ask my mom what lhon and tom krati are, she will say, "Lhon is lhon and tom krati is tom krati." It's not that they can't be defined, but they let you choose your own adventure. Lhon and tom krati are as versatile as they are flavorful. They are dips and gravies, and in Thailand they are essential to our daily life.

But when I say "gravy," it's not like your Italian-American red sauce Sunday gravy or your Thanksgiving gravy. (Would you start dipping cucumbers into your turkey gravy?) These dishes are all things to all people. The combination of their depth of flavor and how easy they are to put together will surprise you. We keep these savory starters in the fridge, and they are what you put out with vegetables before a meal is served, or as an accompaniment to a broader meal, or they are simply served with rice. We also use them on the table as a sort of flavor reset; you can take a bite of them when you are eating other highly flavored foods as a way to cleanse your palate and heighten and expand the flavor of the other dishes.

Nam prik are savory, spicy relishes featured on every Southern Thai table. If you have nam prik in your fridge, you can have it with rice, omelets, and vegetables for an easy and quick meal. Even if I am not hungry, when I see these on the table, I will always eat nam prik. Nam prik are also the building blocks for stir fries such as Moo Kapi (page 164 , Stir-Fried Pork in Shrimp Paste), or soups such as Tom Yum Goong (page 150, Hot and Sour Thai Soup with Shrimp). Shrimp paste and dried shrimp are key in many of these recipes, and remember that some can be saltier than others, so it's important you try it and adapt it to your tastes.

Lhon, nam prik, and tom krati help you find harmony and balance to your meal, and make you enjoy your food more and live a good life.

# NAM PRIK KAPI
## shrimp paste chili relish

MAKES ABOUT ⅔ CUP

Nam prik kapi is a very savory relish, balanced with sweetness. The heat and lime complement each other to add brightness, and the dried shrimp and shrimp paste add that savory hit that makes you want to eat more.

We put it in on the table every day and always keep it in the fridge. We use it as a condiment, like a hot sauce, but I especially love it with raw, crunchy long beans, cabbage, or carrots. It's such an easy way to make a meal with rice or boiled vegetables, an omelet, or a hard-boiled egg, and it's the key flavor in one of my favorite stir-fries, Moo Kapi (page 164). This recipe makes a small amount, but you need just a little bit. Just like you don't need a spoonful of ketchup on your burger, you don't need a lot of nam prik kapi.

All that said, yes, the smell will be strong when you fry the shrimp paste. Enjoy the funky pungent sweetness. But don't burn the shrimp paste because your neighbor might call 911 and you will have to tell them that no one died.

1 In a small skillet or saucepan, heat the oil over medium heat until shimmering-hot, 1 or 2 minutes. Add the shrimp paste patty and cook until it is browned and very fragrant, 1 to 2 minutes per side. Transfer to a plate.

2 Meanwhile, with a mortar and pestle or in a small food processor, pound together or process the brown sugar, shallots, garlic, and chilies until everything is smashed into small pieces. Add the fried shrimp paste, the ground dried shrimp, lime juice, fish sauce, and salt and smash until everything is mixed together. Store the relish in an airtight container in the refrigerator for up to a couple weeks.

3 When you serve it on a dish, garnish it with thinly sliced shallot and thinly sliced Thai chilies.

1 tablespoon canola oil

1 tablespoon shrimp paste, flattened into a patty

3 tablespoons light brown sugar

2 tablespoons thinly sliced shallot (from ½ large)

3 large garlic cloves, peeled but whole

5 Thai chilies, stemmed

1 tablespoon Ground Dried Shrimp (page 137)

5 tablespoons fresh lime juice

½ tablespoon fish sauce

½ teaspoon kosher salt

**GARNISH**

Thinly sliced shallot

Thinly sliced Thai chilies

# NAM PRIK PAO
## mom's chili jam

MAKES 3 CUPS

Nam prik pao is the accessory of the season! Or if you're me, of a lifetime. It is used as both an ingredient in stir-fries or soup like Tom Yum Goong (page 150, Hot and Sour Thai Soup with Shrimp), and as a stand-alone chili jam. This is sweet, sour, and a tiny bit spicy. It's got a sweet heat imparted by the chilies, umami from the dried shrimp, and sour punch from the tamarind. Your house will be fragrant when you make it. *Pao* means "burn," or in this case toasted and charred—the smell of the charring shallots, garlic, and chilies is like a perfume. When I was young, I would make this in a big grinder machine with my mom, and we would make around 110 pounds in one batch! So don't worry about the 3 cups here; you can do it.

My mom has a bold and heavy hand with the dried shrimp, which gives it a very savory flavor. I didn't know about brioche when I was a kid, but now I can tell you to spread it on your brioche and you will thank me.

If we are friends, I will tell you that you can keep it for years in the fridge, but this is America, and we're not friends and you have lawyers, so I'd say it lasts for three months.

4 tablespoons plus ⅓ cup canola or vegetable oil

1 cup thinly sliced shallots

1 cup chopped garlic

2 ounces dried long red chilies, seeded, and cut into 1-inch pieces

7 (70g) discs palm sugar or 1¾ cups brown sugar

¼ cup paprika

¼ cup red chili flakes

¾ cup Ground Dried Shrimp (page 137)

¼ cup fish sauce

½ cup tamarind concentrate (see page 22)

1 tablespoon kosher salt

1  In a nonstick skillet, heat 2 tablespoons of the oil over medium-high heat. Add the shallots, spread them out, and fry, stirring occasionally, until they are charred in spots and evenly golden brown, 5 to 7 minutes. Transfer to a medium bowl.

2  Add 2 more tablespoons of the oil to the skillet and heat over medium-high heat. Add the garlic and spread it out. Cook the garlic, stirring occasionally, until it is charred in spots and golden brown, 3 to 5 minutes. Scrape the garlic and cooking oil into the bowl with the shallots.

3  Pour the remaining ⅓ cup oil into the skillet over medium-high heat and add the dried chilies. Cook, stirring constantly, until the chilies brighten in color, sizzle, and smell fragrant, about 2 minutes. Immediately turn off the heat, remove the chilies with a slotted spoon, and transfer them to a food processor. Keep the oil in the skillet.

4  Add the charred garlic and shallot to the chilies and pulse until everything is finely chopped.

5  Scrape the shallot/garlic/chili mixture into the skillet with the reserved chili oil. Set the skillet over medium-low heat and cook until fragrant, about 1 minute. Add the palm sugar, paprika, and chili flakes. Cook, stirring, until the palm sugar melts. Don't break up the sugar—let it melt at its own pace so everything caramelizes together.

6  Add the ground dried shrimp and stir well. Increase the heat to medium-high, add the fish sauce, and stir for 1 minute. Add the tamarind concentrate and salt and stir for 1 minute.

7  Transfer to a bowl or other heatproof container and let cool completely. Seal and store indefinitely in the refrigerator or freezer.

NOTE: Some packaged dried shrimp is really salty. So if making your own, after you grind it, give it a taste. If the ground dried shrimp tastes really salty, use ½ tablespoon of salt instead of the full tablespoon.

# NAM PRIK SAPAROT
## pineapple chili paste

Nam prik saparot is the centerpiece for your Thai brunch board. It's called a chili paste but it's more of a savory dip, with a base of ground chicken. This is a sweeter nam prik that can be served with long beans, carrots, cucumbers, or any other vegetable to make a very refreshing, savory, satisfying dip. Or spread it on toast! Pineapple adds meaty texture and sweetness and tang. The depth of flavor is bold and rich, and the flavor of tamarind and pineapple flow beautifully together. It's a genius recipe.

2 tablespoons canola oil

1 tablespoon shrimp paste, flattened into a patty

½ tablespoon paprika

2 tablespoons red chili flakes

2½ (70g) discs palm sugar or ½ cup plus 2 tablespoons brown sugar

½ cup thinly sliced shallots

¼ cup finely chopped garlic

½ pound ground chicken

1 cup finely diced fresh pineapple (about ¼ medium pineapple)

2 tablespoons Ground Dried Shrimp (page 137)

¼ cup Thai tamarind concentrate (see page 22)

½ teaspoon kosher salt

2 tablespoons fish sauce

1   In a medium saucepan, heat the oil over medium-high heat. Add the shrimp paste and fry until fragrant and browned, about 1 minute per side. Mash the shrimp paste with a wooden spoon. Then add the paprika and chili flakes and fry until fragrant, about 1 minute.

2   Add the palm sugar, shallot, and garlic. Stir for about 1 minute. Then reduce the heat to medium and keep cooking, stirring frequently, until the palm sugar melts completely (the timing will depend on what form of palm sugar you're using).

3   Add the ground chicken and pineapple and cook, stirring occasionally, until the chicken is cooked through and the pineapple is caramelized, 10 to 15 minutes.

4   Stir in the ground dried shrimp, tamarind concentrate, salt, and fish sauce. Remove the pan from the heat. Store in an airtight container in the fridge for up to a week.

# LHON TAO JIEW
## nok's favorite fermented soybean gravy

There is much more to Thai food than noodles and curry, and I always try to convince people to expand their world. We have many sauces that are not based on curry paste or spices, but that have great flavor. But giving them a term in English can be tricky.

A lhon is a quick and easy "gravy"—maybe that's the easiest way to describe it—and a part of every Southern Thai table; rich and creamy, it complements the heat in the nam prik (relish) you'll probably find on the table as well.

This is a mild coconut citrus gravy with ground pork and shrimp, flavored with Thai fermented soybean paste (you can use miso as a substitute if you have to), and it's a quick and easy lunch to be spooned over rice or served with a lot of raw and boiled vegetables. The contrast of the long hot chilies and the coconut gravy makes a beautiful, colorful sauce, and the mildness makes it kid friendly. The longer you cook it, the better it gets, but even the quickest cooking will make a delicious sauce. Just notice that I call for coconut cream here, not coconut milk; it's much thicker and you won't need to spend time reducing the coconut milk to get the gravy thick and rich.

6 large garlic cloves, smashed

2 tablespoons finely chopped cilantro stems and roots

1¼ cups thinly sliced shallots (2 to 3 large)

2 cups coconut cream

½ cup Thai fermented soybean paste (tao jiew) or ½ cup white miso

½ pound ground pork

8 ounces shrimp, peeled, deveined, and roughly chopped (1 cup)

2 tablespoons sugar

1 teaspoon ground white pepper

½ cup Thai tamarind concentrate (see page 22)

2 tablespoons fish sauce

3 green long hot chilies, sliced ½ inch thick

Thinly sliced red Thai chilies, for garnish

1  With a mortar and pestle or in a small food processor, smash or pulse the garlic, cilantro, and ¼ cup of the shallots until very finely chopped.

2  In a medium saucepan, bring ½ cup of the coconut cream to a boil over medium-high heat. Add the garlic/cilantro/shallot mixture and soybean paste and cook, stirring to break up the paste until fully dissolved.

3  Add the remaining 1½ cups coconut cream, the pork, and shrimp. Bring to a boil and cook, using a wooden spoon to mash the pork into smaller pieces against the sides of the pan until it is fully cooked, about 5 minutes.

4  Stir in the sugar, remaining 1 cup shallots, white pepper, tamarind concentrate, fish sauce, and green chilies and cook for another minute or two, just to make sure everything is heated through. Remove the pan from the heat.

5  Garnish with the prepared chilies.

# LHON PU

## coconut crab gravy *with* fresh vegetables

SERVES 4 TO 6

Get your mortar and pestle ready, because we're about to go pok-pok-pok to smash up aromatics for a beautiful, luxurious coconut and crab gravy with salted egg yolks. Normally we use crab roe for this recipe, but salted egg yolk is the closest thing we have in North America that adds a similar depth of flavor, so that is what I use. While we're talking about substitutions, you can use a food processor instead of the mortar and pestle, too.

This lhon is very beautiful, very luxurious. The flavors are creamy and subtle, and it's an umami bomb that will make you feel good. Like all the recipes in this section, pair this with fresh raw or blanched vegetables (it's delicious with green apples too!), spicy nam priks, and rice.

2 tablespoons canola or vegetable oil

6 salted egg yolks

6 large garlic cloves, smashed and peeled

2 tablespoons finely chopped cilantro stems and roots

1¼ cups thinly sliced shallots (2 to 3 large)

2 cups coconut cream

1 cup lump crabmeat

2 tablespoons sugar

½ to 1 teaspoon kosher salt

1 teaspoon ground white pepper

2 tablespoons fish sauce

½ cup Thai tamarind concentrate (see page 22)

2 red long hot chilies, thinly sliced on the diagonal

Handful of cilantro leaves, chopped

1   Line a plate with paper towels and set near the stove. In a small skillet or saucepan, heat the oil over high heat. When it smokes, add the salted egg yolks and fry, turning them frequently, until they are evenly browned, 2 to 3 minutes. Transfer the egg yolks to the paper towels and let them cool slightly, then crumble them into small pieces. You should have about ½ cup.

2   With a mortar and pestle or in a small food processor, smash or pulse the garlic, cilantro, and ¼ cup of the shallots until very finely chopped.

3   In a medium saucepan, bring ½ cup of the coconut cream to a boil over medium-high heat. Add the garlic/cilantro/shallot mixture and cook for a minute or so, until fragrant. Add the remaining 1½ cups coconut cream and the remaining 1 cup shallots and cook for 2 minutes. Reduce the heat to medium and add the crumbled egg yolks, crabmeat, sugar, salt, white pepper, fish sauce, and tamarind concentrate. Cook for 2 to 3 minutes to heat everything through and meld the flavors.

4   Remove from the heat and stir in the chilies and cilantro.

# NHOR MAI TOM KRATI

**bamboo shoots cooked in coconut milk–shrimp paste sauce**

SERVES 4 TO 6

You will not be able to stop eating this, as the delicate creaminess of the coconut is infused with garlic, shallot, shrimp paste, and dried shrimp. You can find the Japanese bamboo shoots in the grocery store precooked in a sealed package, and these are wonderful and so easy. Bamboo shoots are similar to palm hearts; they add a mellow earthiness. But do yourself a favor and do *not* use fresh bamboo shoots, or it will take forever to cook.

Pair this with your favorite spicy nam prik, and raw and boiled vegetables, and of course rice.

- 3 cups canned coconut milk
- 3 large garlic cloves, smashed and peeled
- ½ large shallot, thinly sliced (¼ cup)
- 1 tablespoon shrimp paste
- ¼ cup dried shrimp
- 1 pound precooked bamboo shoots, halved lengthwise and sliced ¼ inch thick
- 2 tablespoons sugar
- 1 tablespoon fish sauce

In a medium saucepan, combine the coconut milk, garlic, shallot, shrimp paste, and dried shrimp. Bring to a boil over medium-high heat, stirring constantly and mashing the shrimp paste against the sides of the pan until it is fully dissolved. Add the sliced bamboo shoots, sugar, and fish sauce and cook for 2 or 3 more minutes to heat everything through and meld the flavors.

# LHON PLA KEM
## salted fish & tuna gravy

SERVES 4 TO 6

In the old days, canned fish like salmon or tuna was the most exciting thing to be able to use in a recipe. It was considered a luxurious item, since it was European—foreign and therefore valuable—and it was only for people with money. But dried, salted fish is something that every Thai person has in their pantry. In Southern Thailand, we eat salted fish a lot because it's the traditional way of preserving fish before refrigerators, and because the salting process creates a lot of umami and has a pungent flavor that we love. Plus, in our cuisine, when we eat spicy food, salt helps balance the flavor. We have salted fish in every form, small and tiny like anchovy, and big like king mackerel. It adds dimension into your food and completes your meal.

Now that you know more about salted fish, maybe you will think it's as foreign and exciting as we thought canned tuna was. I'll help you with a recipe that marries both these kinds of preserved fish in a coconut gravy with chilies, herbs, and pepper. It's salty, but balanced and delicious with rice and vegetables.

When handling salted fish, your hands will be very smelly, so wear some gloves, or they will be pungent for a while. Wash your hands 20 times; washing with a slice of lime helps.

3 cups canned coconut milk

2 cups thinly sliced shallots (about 3 large)

2 tablespoons finely chopped garlic (5 or 6 large cloves)

2 tablespoons finely chopped cilantro stems

¼ cup finely chopped or crumbled salted mackerel

2 (5-ounce) cans oil-packed tuna, drained

½ tablespoon freshly ground black pepper

½ tablespoon ground white pepper

1 tablespoon light brown sugar

½ cup Thai tamarind concentrate (see page 22)

½ to 1 teaspoon kosher salt

1 tablespoon fish sauce

5 makrut lime leaves

10 Thai chilies, smashed

2 red long hot chilies, thinly sliced

½ cup chopped fresh cilantro

1  In a medium saucepan, bring ½ cup of the coconut milk to a boil over high heat. Add 1 cup of the shallots, the garlic, cilantro stems, and salted mackerel. Cook for 2 minutes, stirring with a wooden spoon. Add the canned tuna and mash it up with the spoon. Add the remaining 2½ cups coconut milk, the black pepper, and white pepper and stir well. Let it come to a boil, reduce the heat to medium, and keep cooking for 8 to 10 minutes to thicken the sauce.

2  Stir in the remaining 1 cup shallots, the brown sugar, tamarind concentrate, salt, and fish sauce. Cook for 5 minutes or so. Stir in the lime leaves, Thai chilies, long hots, and cilantro and remove from the heat.

# KHANOM WAN

**Thai desserts are all-day snacks, not overly sweet and heavy ends to a meal.**

They are colorful and delicately crafted in a way that makes people feel satisfied and happy. They are affordable and accessible in the market, and range in flavor from subtle sweetness to bright and zesty. We use the natural sugars of ingredients that grow all around us, like coconut, lime, and durian.

While the range of Thai sweets can easily fill a whole cookbook on their own, this chapter includes a few simple recipes that feature a balanced sweetness from fruit, coconut, and the gentle taste of rice. These desserts are not labor-intensive, and the fresh and seasonal ingredients make them shine.

You can make these desserts for a dinner party or to have on hand any time you want a happy pick-me-up during the day. Thai desserts are a warm welcome, a shared smile, and a display of appreciation for what our garden and market can offer us.

# KHAO NIEW TURIAN
## durian sticky rice

You are sophisticated. You are smart. You are bold. So don't tell me you don't like durian fruit. Yes, it's a fact that durian isn't allowed in hotels and public transport because of its pungent sweet smell, but that should not make you fear the king of all fruits. It's glorious for many reasons, and you will have severe FOMO if you skip the opportunity to try it. The way I love to introduce people to durian is with this dish, paired with chewy sticky rice soaked in sweetened coconut milk with a salty coconut cream topping.

Don't bother buying fresh durian. It's expensive and it's hard to know what's good. The quality of frozen durian is amazing, because it is frozen at its peak freshness and is conveniently seeded. When you try durian at its peak, the delicate, creamy-sweet and funky finish makes you feel alive. And it's extremely nutritious, with lots of potassium, vitamin C, iron, and antioxidants. You don't need to take a vitamin, just eat durian.

And yes, it may look like a lot of salt in this recipe, but it's necessary to balance the flavors of this beautiful dessert. The salinity offsets the funkiness and brightens the sweet creaminess of the coconut milk and rice.

### RICE

Sticky Rice (page 236)

2 cups canned coconut milk

1½ cups granulated sugar

2 to 3 teaspoons kosher salt

1 pandan leaf, cut into long, thin strips and tied together in a knot

### TOPPING

1½ cups coconut cream

2 to 3 teaspoons kosher salt

1 cup thawed frozen durian, diced

1   Make the rice: Soak and steam the rice as directed. Transfer the cooked rice to a heatproof bowl.

2   Meanwhile, in a medium saucepan, combine the coconut milk, sugar, salt, and knotted pandan leaf. Cook over high heat, stirring, until the coconut milk comes to a boil, then remove it from the heat. Make sure not to cook it for too long, or the oil in the coconut milk will separate.

3   Pour the hot coconut milk mixture over the sticky rice. It will look soupy: do not panic. Cover the bowl with plastic wrap or a lid and set aside for 5 minutes. Stir the rice, smooth it out, then cover it again and let it sit for 5 more minutes. The sticky rice will be creamy. Stir well.

4   Make the topping: In a small saucepan, bring the coconut cream to a boil. Add the salt and take the pan off the heat. When the coconut cream has cooled slightly, stir in the durian. The durian is sweet like a hug from Nok.

5   Spoon the sticky rice into bowls and top with the durian/coconut cream mixture.

# KHAO NIEW MA MUANG
## mango sticky rice

SERVES 6

This is the most beloved and requested Thai dessert at my restaurant. It also is a snack and can be eaten on its own. The key here is that the mangoes must be of great quality and at peak ripeness, sweetness, and aroma for the dish to have a perfect balance. The rice grains should be soft, glossy, and creamy; the coconut cream should not be overly sweet, and the mango should be smooth, not stringy and fibrous.

I serve this at my restaurant only when the mangoes are great, and a lot of that has to do with how they're grown, picked, and handled. But you can help them along by letting them ripen. Normally when you find a mango, you can leave it on the countertop until it gets crinkly and really sweet, almost to the point that it's overripe. Brown spots usually mean it's really sweet and you can cut the brown spots off if you don't like how they look. You can leave it in a paper bag in a dark place—and in Thailand we put it in a rice bucket. Unfortunately, some mangoes never really ripen and get sweet, or are fibrous. Use those in your smoothies.

Sticky Rice (page 236)
2 cups canned coconut milk
1½ cups granulated sugar
2 to 3 teaspoons kosher salt
1 pandan leaf, cut into long, thin strips and tied together in a knot

**TOPPING**
1½ cups coconut cream
2 tablespoons rice flour
2 to 3 teaspoons kosher salt
3 ripe medium mangoes, sliced
Sesame seeds (optional), for topping

1 **Make the rice:** Soak and steam the rice as directed. Transfer the cooked rice to a heatproof bowl.

2 Meanwhile, in a medium saucepan, combine the coconut milk, sugar, salt, and knotted pandan leaf. Cook over high heat, stirring, until the coconut milk comes to a boil. Then remove it from the heat.

3 Pour the hot coconut milk mixture over the sticky rice. It will look soupy: do not panic. Cover the bowl with plastic wrap or a lid and set aside for 5 minutes. Stir the rice, smooth it out, then cover it again and let it sit for 5 more minutes. The rice will be creamy. Stir well.

4 **Make the topping:** In a small saucepan, whisk together the coconut cream, rice flour, and salt. Set over medium heat and cook, whisking constantly, until thickened. Remove from the heat and set aside.

5 Top each serving of sticky rice with some sliced mango, a sprinkle of sesame seeds (if using), and a drizzle of the coconut cream mixture.

# KHAO NIEW DUM

## black rice pudding *with* coconut cream and longan

**SERVES 6**

Most cultures have a version of rice pudding. Thais normally don't serve this dish after dinner; we usually serve it all day because it's a snack we can grab in the market. This recipe calls for black sticky rice, which is sweet and high in fiber; it's healthier than other rice and has a wonderful bite to it. The rice is almost a rich dark purple when you cook it down and it becomes glossy and beautiful. There is something magical about using rice as a dessert. The grain is so versatile.

Longan fruit is considered a superfood in North America, where it is thought to restore sleep, reduce anxiety, and relieve a host of other ailments. It's available fresh or canned at most Asian markets. The flavor is sweet with a juicy, chewy texture, similar to lychee but even sweeter. We eat this all the time in Thailand because it grows abundantly and is healthy and joyful.

**RICE**

1 cup black sticky rice, soaked in water overnight at room temperature

¾ cup granulated sugar

½ to 1 teaspoon kosher salt

1 (20-ounce) can longan in syrup

**TOPPING**

1 cup coconut cream

½ to 1 teaspoon kosher salt

1 tablespoon rice flour

1  **Make the rice:** Drain the rice. In a medium saucepan, combine the rice and 4 cups water. Bring to a boil over high heat, then reduce the heat to low and cook, stirring occasionally, until almost tender, about 30 minutes.

2  Stir in the sugar and salt and increase the heat to medium-high. Cook, stirring frequently, until the liquid evaporates, 3 to 5 minutes. Add the longan with its syrup and cook, stirring, for 30 seconds to 1 minute. Remove from the heat.

3  **Make the topping:** In a small saucepan, whisk together the coconut cream, salt, and rice flour. Cook over medium heat, whisking, until thickened, 2 to 4 minutes. Remove from the heat.

4  Scoop the rice pudding into individual bowls and top with the coconut cream.

# NOK'S VANILLA COCONUT MILK PANNA COTTA WITH PINEAPPLE

SERVES 6

Ask yourself: Do you want to feel confident today and do you want to make beautiful food? This panna cotta is so easy people with no baking skills can make it. If you want a bright, citrusy, sweet pop of flavor and a creamy custard that looks like you are on a competitive cooking show, this is for you.

Just make sure you prepare it the night before serving so the panna cotta can set into a beautiful custard.

Even if you don't know how to boil water, you can make this dish. (You just have to know how to simmer.)

### PANNA COTTA

4 silver gelatin sheets (about 2.5 grams each, see Note)

2½ cups canned coconut milk

½ cup sugar (100 grams)

Pinch to ¼ teaspoon kosher salt

Grated zest of 1 lime

### TOPPING

½ medium pineapple, peeled, cored, and finely diced (2 cups)

Juice of ½ lime

¼ cup sugar

Pinch of kosher salt

1 vanilla bean

**NOTE:** Silver gelatin might sound fancy, but it's easy and fun to use. You can find it easily online—"silver" is a grade of strength, so make sure you don't buy a different grade.

1 **Make the panna cotta:** Soak the gelatin sheets in a bowl of cold water for 5 minutes. (This lets them "bloom.") Drain the gelatin, squeeze it, and pat it gently with paper towels to get rid of excess water. Make sure it is completely dry and discard the water.

2 In a medium saucepan, combine the coconut milk, sugar, and salt. Bring to a simmer over medium heat, and simmer for 5 minutes to thicken a bit. (Reduce the heat to medium-low if it looks like the coconut milk will boil.) Remove the pan from the heat and stir in the gelatin and 1 teaspoon lime zest.

3 Divide the mixture among six 6-ounce ramekins. Cover and refrigerate overnight.

4 **Make the topping:** In a bowl, combine the pineapple, remaining lime zest, lime juice, sugar, and salt. Split the vanilla bean open and scrape in the vanilla seeds. Toss everything together.

5 Spoon the pineapple mixture on top of each ramekin and serve. Or, if you want to be fancy, run a sharp knife around the edges of each panna cotta. Then dip the bottom of the ramekins in hot water, invert the panna cottas onto plates, and top with the pineapple mixture.

# MENUS

Here are some suggested menus for creating your own Southern Thai table. These menus are meant to help you understand the range of the Southern Thai table and how we pair dishes so that their different flavors and textures complement one another. You don't have to cook every recipe on the menu, it's up to you, but you can build your confidence by trying a few dishes from each menu over time.

## MENU 1: **Mom's Table**

My mom would make beautiful meals for us after a long day of working at her market stall. My mom's table menu is nutritious and satisfying and showcases the depth of flavor in our curries and braises. Enjoy the way the sourness of a sour curry complements the sweetness of the braised pork belly and how the baked salted fish makes the other dishes pop.

Gaeng Som Pak Tai (page 118, Sour Curry with Shrimp and Pineapple)

Moo Hong (page 228, Braised Pork Belly)

Kana Pla Kem (page 172, Chinese Broccoli with Salted Fish)

Kalum Thod Nam Pla (page 186, Three-Ingredient Cabbage)

Sauces:
Kapi Sauce (page 167, Shrimp Paste Sauce) and Prik Nam Pla (page 42, Fish Sauce and Chili Condiment)

## MENU 2: **Nok's Table**

This is what I will cook for you when you come to my house. These are the meals I love to eat and love to cook. They are all quick to prepare, and with a little planning in the morning, you will have a showstopper meal at night. The basil tofu and mushroom, turmeric fish, and glass noodle salad will all come together in no time. The red curry with prawns needs a bit of focus, and you may need a little more prep for the pork-stuffed tapioca pearls, or you can have your guests stuff the dumpling wrappers with you while you drink your wine or seltzer.

Gaeng Kua Goong Lychee (page 131, Red Curry with Prawns, Cherry Tomatoes, and Lychees)

Yum Woon Sen Talay/Moo Saap (page 89, Glass Noodle Salad with Shrimp, Pork, and Squid)

Sakoo Sai Moo (page 75, Pork-Stuffed Tapioca Pearls)

Pla Kamin (page 163, Turmeric Fish)

Tao Hu Pad Hor Ra Pa Hed (page 184, Basil Tofu and Mushroom)

Sauce: Nam Prik Kapi (page 255, Shrimp Paste Chili Relish)

## MENU 3: **Intro to Southern Thai Food**

This is Southern Thai 101. If you can manage this menu, no doubt you will graduate with honors from this cookbook. (Wouldn't it be nice if real life were this easy?) All of these recipes are quick and profile a range of Southern Thai flavors, from our warming spices in five-spice eggs to our heavy-handed love of garlic in garlic chicken.

Khai Pa Lo Hed (page 245, Five-Spice Egg and Mushrooms with Tofu)

Gai Pad Kratiem (page 171, Garlic and Black Pepper Chicken)

Pad Ma Kua Yaow (page 180, My Mother's Colorful Stir-Fried Eggplant)

Sauce: Prik Nam Pla (page 42, Fish Sauce and Chili Condiment)

## MENU 4: **Kid Friendly**

Does your child live on a diet of string cheese and yogurt pouches? Expand their world with these comforting and beloved recipes. Crab fried rice and steamed eggs with ground pork and salted egg yolk are mild and delicate, and the tofu and pineapple curry is an introduction to spice balanced by the sweetness of pineapple. I promise you, kids will enjoy these meals and ask you to make them again. Host a playdate and invite everyone to enjoy this feast. Did anyone say you are a good parent today? You are doing great.

Kang Jued Woon Sen (page 154, Pork Meatball Soup and Glass Noodles with Fried Garlic Oil)

Khao Pad Pu (page 238, Egg and Crab Fried Rice)

Khai Toon Moo Sub (page 252, Steamed Eggs with Ground Pork and Salted Egg Yolk)

Gaeng Pajari (page 128, Seared Tofu and Pineapple Coconut Curry)

Nam Prik Saparot (page 258, Pineapple Chili Paste)

Sauce: Prik Nam Pla (page 42, Fish Sauce and Chili Condiment)

## MENU 5: **Bright and Comforting**

Cook this menu when you need a pick-me-up on a bad day. The green curry with beef is creamy, vibrant, and comforting, and the familiar tastes of stuffed Thai eggs will make you feel at ease. My mother's chicken soup will warm your senses and make everyone feel like they are getting taken care of by my mom.

Gaeng Kiew Waan Osso Buco (page 127, Green Curry with Beef Shanks)

Green Coconut Rice (page 235)

Khai Yud Saai (page 251, Pi Goong's and Pi Kul's Stuffed Egg Crepes)

Gai Tom Kamin (page 149, My Mother's Turmeric Chicken Soup for a Cold)

## MENU 6: **Date Night**

Spice up your romantic life and impress your date with this menu. A spicy eggplant salad and baked mussels with herbs are both familiar and adventurous in their herbaceous and earthy flavors with a pop of heat. Fall in love over the delicate flavors of mango sticky rice, and don't forget the amazing meal that brought you closer together.

Hoi Mang Phu Ob Samun Prai (page 227, Baked Mussels with Herbs)

Yum Ma Kuer Yao (page 101, Spicy Eggplant Salad with Chili Jam and Coconut Cream)

Khao Niew Ma Muang (page 274, Mango Sticky Rice)

Sauce: Nam Jim Seafood (page 34, Seafood Sauce) and Nam Jim Jaew (page 38, Charred Aromatic Tamarind Chili Dipping Sauce)

## MENU 7: **Casual Dinner Party**

Relax and have fun cooking for your friends and family with these sharp and vibrant recipes. This menu showcases a range of flavors from the sharp brightness of black pepper in the glass noodles to the umami-laden heat of dry red curry and mushrooms. The salt in Chinese broccoli with salted fish balances the meal out and heightens the flavors.

Goong Ob Woonsen (page 223, My Mother's Acclaimed Baked Shrimp with Glass Noodles)

Pad Prik King Hed (page 135, Dry Red Curry with Pan-Fried Tofu and Mushrooms)

Kana Pla Kem (page 172, Chinese Broccoli with Salted Fish)

Sauce: Nam Prik Saparot (page 258, Pineapple Chili Paste)

## MENU 8: **Fancy Dinner Party (An All-6-Burner Event)**

Have you been watching too much *Chef's Table*? Want to get in touch with your inner Nok? Sharpen your knives and get ready to immerse yourself in the beauty of using ingredients from the garden, farm, and sea. None of these recipes is particularly difficult, but they will take a day's worth of prep work to make all together. Consider this your Southern Thai Thanksgiving.

Khao Niew Luang Nah Goong (page 241, Yellow Sticky Rice with Shrimp)

Nok's Chicken Massaman Curry (page 122)

Goong Pad Nam Prik Phao (page 179, Shrimp and Chili Jam Stir-Fry)

Pad Pak Kad Dong (page 183, Comforting Pickled Mustard Greens with Eggs)

Mieng Pla Thod (page 193, Fried Branzino with Herbs)

Lhon Pu (page 262, Coconut Crab Gravy with Fresh Vegetables)

Nok's Vanilla Coconut Milk Panna Cotta with Pineapple (page 277)

Sauce: Prik Nam Pla (page 42, Fish Sauce and Chili Condiment), Nam Jim Seafood (page 34, Seafood Sauce), Nam Pla Waan Pak Chee (page 37, Palm Sugar and Fish Sauce Relish with Fried Garlic and Shallots)

## MENU 9: **Easy Weekend Feast**

You don't always need a challenging weekend project, but if you want a feast without a ton of work, you need this easy weekend meal. These recipes are great to cook on a Saturday morning and have around to feed your family all weekend. All of the recipes are mild and satisfying and keep well in the fridge.

Yum Nua (page 91, Steak Salad with Toasted Rice Powder)

Soup Hang Wua (page 157, Nok's Childhood Oxtail Soup with Herbs and Crispy Shallots)

Khao Mun Gai (page 73, Chicken and Rice)

Sauce: Nam Jim Tao Jiew (page 33, Fermented Bean Sauce), Nam Jim Seafood (page 34, Seafood Sauce), and Prik Dong (page 42, Chili and Vinegar Relish)

# THANK YOU / ขอบคุณค่ะ

This book is for my mother, Kalaya. For everything she taught me and everything she has done. She is my inspiration and she made me who I am. She shaped me into the person I am today, and I want her to be proud.

Thank you to everyone who made this book possible.

Ziv is my number one cheerleader, who I unconditionally love and who always supports me.

My team: Natalie Jesionka, Peggy Paul Casella, and Michael Persico.

My beloved Tong and Titi, who always support me and comfort me.

My neighbors who always are my guinea pigs when we want someone to taste the recipes.

My team at Kalaya, who help me with recipes and keep the ship going.

Kru Padung for sharing his wisdom and style so the recipes always live on.

David Black and Francis Lam for guiding this amazing project and believing Southern Thai food should be shared with the world.

## NATALIE

Thank you to Nok for filling the kitchen with laughter and inspiration. Every day of this process was the best day.

Thanks to Peggy and Mike for their vibrancy and expertise.

Thanks to Francis Lam for all the support. I learned so much from your reflective inquiry.

Thanks to David Black and Rica Allannic for their guidance and encouragement.

Thanks to Ash and Asher for their love and shared zeal for eating Nok's food.

Thanks to my family: Ania, Mike, Jen, and Mikey for all your love, support, and patience during those years I traversed the world. It has finally come full circle.

## MIKE

Infinite thanks to Nok for deciding that we would take this wild and exciting journey together to the other end of the world. Thank you for trusting me to tell your story through these photographs. What a fantastic journey it has been.

To the indelible Thailand family—thanks to Bright, Nick, Kay, Kru Padung, and Kalaya for welcoming me so warmly to Thailand. It was an incredible experience, made even more remarkable thanks to you.

To Kelsi and Ed—thank you so much for your talent and care and for making our stateside recipe shoot so special.

To Lizzy—your love, support, and patience is forever appreciated; Nok and I cannot thank you enough for your help getting these hundreds of images into their right place.

To my family—as I travel, I cannot help but be thankful for all that you've taught me; most important, to share food and good times with friends and family (new and old) as much as humanly possible . . . not much else matters.

Love to all.

## PEGGY

Thanks to Nok for changing the way I look at and play with flavors, for taking my spice tolerance to new heights, and for sharing her incredible talent and personality with me (and the world).

Thanks to Natalie and Mike for their artistry and incredible talents, and to the team at Clarkson Potter for helping us create a book that reflects the beauty and liveliness of Nok's food.

And, finally, thanks to my husband, John; son, Jack; and neighbors who helped me devour testing day leftovers.

# INDEX

Library of Congress Cataloging-in-
Publication Data
Names: Suntaranon, Nok, author. |
  Jesionka, Natalie, author. | Persico,
  Michael, photographer.
Title: Kalaya's Southern Thai kitchen / Nok
  Suntaranon with Natalie
  Jesionka ; photographs by Michael
  Persico.
Description: New York : Clarkson Potter/
  Publisher, [2024] | Includes index.
  | Identifiers: LCCN 2023053463 (print) |
  LCCN 2023053464 (ebook) | ISBN
  9780593580875 (hardcover) | ISBN
  9780593580882 (ebook)
Subjects: LCSH: Kalaya Restaurant
  | Cooking, Thai. | Restaurants—
  Philadelphia. | LCGFT: Cookbooks.
Classification: LCC TX724.5.T5 S865 2024
  (print) | LCC TX724.5.T5  (ebook)
  | DDC 641.59593—dc23/eng/20231220
LC record available at https://lccn.loc.
  gov/2023053463
LC ebook record available at https://lccn.
  loc.gov/2023053464

ISBN 978-0-593-58087-5
Ebook ISBN 978-0-593-58088-2

Printed in China

Editor: Francis Lam
Editorial assistant: Darian Keels
Designer: Stephanie Huntwork
Production editor: Abby Oladipo
Production manager: Phil Leung
Compositors: Merri Ann Morrell
and Zoe Tokushige
Stylists: Vippittichek Nick Pitthayanont
and Tikhamporn Chuenkittivoravat
Food and prop stylist: Kelsi Windmiller
Wardrobe: Malinee by Tirawan
Pangsrivongse
Photo assistants: Peerarat "Bright"
Thaingamsi and Edward Newton
Photo retoucher: Taylor Saya Shaw
Recipe developer: Peggy Paul Casella
Copyeditor: Kate Slate
Proofreaders: Nancy Inglis, Penny Haynes,
and Alisa Garrison
Indexer: Elizabeth Parson
Publicist: Lauren Chung
Marketer: Chloe Aryeh

10 9 8 7 6 5 4 3 2 1

First Edition